University of

———— MIND MATTERS ————

minds, brains and machines

——MIND MATTERS——

Series editor: Judith Hughes

In the same series

————— MIND MATTERS —————

minds, brains and machines

GEOFFREY BROWN

PUBLISHED BY BRISTOL CLASSICAL PRESS

To my family

First published in 1989 by
Bristol Classical Press
an imprint of
Gerald Duckworth & Co. Ltd
The Old Piano Factory
48 Hoxton Square, London N1 6PB

Reprinted with corrections and Index, 1997

A catalogue record for this book is available
from the British Library

ISBN 1-85399-013-2

Available in USA and Canada from:
Focus Information Group
PO Box 369
Newburyport
MA 01950

Printed in Great Britain by
Booksprint, Bristol

contents

preface to the second edition

Since this book first appeared, I have been pleasantly surprised by the feedback which I have received from readers who have found it useful as an introduction in this area of philosophy; my thanks to all who have made constructive comments, some of which have been incorporated in the present edition.

bibliographical note

In addition to original suggestions for further reading, the following more recent publications are strongly recommended:

D. Dennett, *Consciousness Explained* (Harmondsworth: Penguin, 1991).
Velmans, M. (ed.), *The Science of Consciousness* [a collection of essays] (London: Routledge, 1996)

foreword

'A philosophical problem has the form *I don't know my way about*,' said Wittgenstein. These problems are not the ones where we need information, but those where we are lost for lack of adequate signposts and landmarks. Finding our way – making sense out of the current confusions and becoming able to map things both for ourselves and for others – is doing successful philosophy. This is not quite what the lady meant who told me when I was seven that I ought to have more philosophy, because philosophy was eating up your cabbage and not making a fuss about it. But that lady *was* right to suggest that there were some useful skills here.

Philosophizing, then, is not just a form of highbrow chess for postgraduate students; it is becoming conscious of the shape of our lives, and anybody may need to do it. Our culture contains an ancient tradition which is rich in helpful ways of doing so, and in Europe they study that tradition at school. Here, that study is at present being squeezed out even from university courses. But that cannot stop us doing it if we want to. This series contains excellent guide-books for people who do want to, guide-books which are clear, but which are not superficial surveys. They are themselves pieces of real philosophy, directed at specific problems which are likely to concern all of us. Read them.

MARY MIDGLEY

preface

Philosophers are very good at talking to one another. Some of them are also good at talking with other people. In the market-places of Athens, the cafés of Paris, and lately, in the pubs of London, philosophers have always found a public bursting with its own ideas and keen to discuss them with others. The need to ask and attempt to answer philosophical questions is in us all and is prompted sometimes by particular events in our personal lives and sometimes by a more general unease about wider social or political or scientific issues. At such times there is always a popular demand for philosophers to explain themselves and the views of their illustrious forebears in ways which others can understand and question and use.

It is not an easy thing to do because Philosophy is not easy, though its central insights, like those in the sciences, are often startlingly simple. To gain those insights we all have to follow the paths of reasoning for ourselves. Signposts have been left for us by the great philosophers of the past, and deciphering some of them is part of the business of this series.

'Mind Matters' is not 'Philosophy Made Easy' but rather 'Philosophy Made Intelligible', and the authors in this series have been chosen for more than their philosophical knowledge. Some of them are also experts in other fields such as medicine, computing or biology. All are people who recognise and try to practise the art of writing in an accessible and clear manner, believing that philosophical thought which is not understandable is best kept to oneself. Many have acquired this ability in the harsh discipline of adult education where students bring their own knowledge and puzzles to the subject and demand real explanations of relevant issues.

Each book in this series begins with a perplexing question that we may ask ourselves without, perhaps, realising that we are 'philosophising': Do computers have minds? Can a pile of bricks be a work of art? Should we hold pathological killers responsible for their crimes? Such questions are considered and new questions raised with frequent reference to the views of major philosophers. The authors go further than this, however. It is not their intention to produce a potted history of philosophical ideas. They also make their own contributions to the subject, suggesting different avenues of thought to explore. The result is a collection of original writings on a wide range of topics produced for all those who find Philosophy as fascinating and compelling as they do.

Whether or not machines can think is the stuff of which dreams and nightmares are made. Geoffrey Brown lives in this world, however, and his expertise in computing engineering gives him a down-to-earth view of the present complexity and future possibilities of the machines which appear to control much of our lives.

But he is also a philosopher who sees that the question demands careful consideration of some fundamental issues. What do we mean by 'think'? Is machine 'thinking' like human 'thinking'? What does it mean to be conscious? And in answering these questions we reach the heart of what is called the philosophy of mind.

JUDITH HUGHES

vii

acknowledgements

I am happy to express my thanks to the Catholic University of Leuven, Belgium, for the fellowship during the course of which this book was written, and to all the members of the Institute of Philosophy who gave me help and encouragement, especially Herman De Dijn and Herman Roelants. Special thanks are also due to Frank Bock for assistance in innumerable ways. I am grateful for many useful discussions with Geoffrey Midgley and for helpful suggestions from Mary Midgley and from David Bell. I am grateful also to my wife Valerie for her help and support.

introduction

'Can a machine think – that is, really think in the same sense that human beings really think?' This is a question which most people are by now quite used to hearing from various quarters. It is not just an obscure 'philosopher's question', in the sense of a question which is of interest only to a small and specialised bunch of academics – though it is indeed a philosophical question, and our treatment of it will be an exercise in Philosophy. Nor is such a question of interest purely to those whose work lies in the field now known as Artificial Intelligence. Today a large and ever increasing number of people come into contact with highly sophisticated machines, either in the course of their job or of a pastime. People make use of them, interrogate them, compete with them in games, talk to them, and often love them or hate them – or even both.

It is hardly surprising, therefore, that the question should arise for people of how far these machines can be, or ought to be, treated as actually thinking, genuinely intelligent, creatures. For it is clear that they are capable of many of the same intellectual tasks that human beings are able to perform. Furthermore, if someone is unable to believe that genuine thought is going on inside his common-or-garden desktop computer, do there not exist machines many times more powerful and complex, to which real thought could nevertheless be attributed? And if even this doesn't look too promising, the way has now been opened for him to ask the question: 'Could any man-made machine ever, in principle, be said to be thinking in the full sense?'

1

People interrogate them, compete with them in games...

Now once a question of this kind really takes hold of us, once we have really understood its implications, it tends to hang around in our minds and refuse to leave until it gets an answer. This, it might be said, is characteristic of a philosophical problem, or perhaps of a philosopher. A relatively unreflective person will typically throw at it the first answer that comes into his head: 'Of course they can't – they could never do this-that-or-the-other'; 'Obviously they can, they already do such-and-such far faster than the human brain!' We have probably all heard these glib responses. It may be said here that if anyone thinks the question posed above is indeed a trivial or stupid one, or that it can be answered in a few words only, then he had better stop reading at this point, unless he is prepared to consider that things might be otherwise. For it is ultimately with this question that we shall be concerned throughout this book.

There are at least two ways of going about getting to a chosen destination (in this case, an answer to the question). One is simply to make a bee-line for it, ignoring everything else in sight, and possibly thereby missing a great many landmarks that might have been of use. Another is to approach it in a more leisurely and open-minded fashion, stopping where there is something of interest, viewing the scenery and noting the intersections with adjacent routes, and maybe even asking ourselves occasionally whether the original destination was where we should really have aimed at in the first place. It is something like this latter approach which will be adopted in what follows. The reader must not, therefore, be put off if some of the ground covered seems at the time to be only loosely connected with the topic in hand, or even downright irrelevant. It is hard to know in advance what considerations will prove relevant to solving a philosophical problem, for it is also fairly typical of a philosophical question that there is some unclarity regarding what sort of a question it actually is. Is it, for example, a matter of observation and experience, of calculation, of pure reasoning, or perhaps merely of definition?

Moreover, philosophical questions tend to need a context. Such questions do not come simply 'out of the blue'. And the context of the particular question which we have set ourselves here, is the whole tradition of what is called the Philosophy of Mind, at least in the modern period, which by general consent is reckoned as dating from the seventeenth century. It is therefore part of the purpose of the book to convey to the reader something, though it will be a small taste only, of the flavour of that tradition.

Having said a little about the nature of philosophical questions, we may now consider briefly how philosophical questions are answered. The activity of philosophy does not consist, as some academic pursuits do, in the collecting of facts, or the presentation merely of pieces of information. A philo-sophical problem can only properly be approached by conducting an argument; that is, by seeing how a number of considerations, which may in themselves be quite mundane and familiar, are connected. Argument, in this sense, need not necessarily mean arguing against anyone, or the taking of sides in a disagreement. All that is necessary is the existence of a conceptual problem, and the ability to make out a reasoned case in favour of one particular answer, or type of answer, to it.

With this in mind, let us run briefly through the way in which the argument will proceed in the remainder of this book.

After some initial clarification in *chapter 1*, we will go on in *chapter 2* to discuss the ways in which the presence or absence of thought can be recognised in general – as much in human beings as in machines. We will find that this raises some awkward questions about the evidence for other minds.

In *chapter 3* the Problem of Other Minds (what makes one think that anything, apart from oneself, has real thoughts?) will be met head-on. Attempts to solve the problem on the part of various previous philosophers will be discussed, but no definitive solution will be offered at this stage.

A solution of a kind will, however, be presented in *chapter 4*, in which we look at the philosophy of Ludwig Wittgenstein, and in particular the celebrated 'Private Language Argument'. This will, we shall find, throw light also on the kind of symptoms of genuine thought for which we should be looking.

In *chapter 5* the topic of communication in relation to the capacity for thought will be discussed, and we will be looking at one or two examples of the ways in which computers can be made to interact with people in something like the same way that human beings do.

Chapters 6, 7 and *8* will be devoted to examining a range of traditional approaches to the 'Mind-Body Problem' – that is, the philosophical problem concerning the relationship between the physical and mental features of human beings. Only by doing this can we get a clear picture of what we think the relationship would be, if any, between a machine's ability to think, and its physical make-up.

Continuing from there, *chapter 9* will go into a little more technical detail (though not too much) regarding both computers and the human brain, and will ask the question: are there enough significant similarities to make us suspect that real thought in one may imply real thought in the other?

In *chapter 10*, some arguments will be presented concerning the relations between a cluster of concepts which we will by then have encountered: thought, conceptualization, rule-following, purposiveness, autonomy, and consciousness.

Finally, *chapter 11* will embody such conclusions as we are able to reach in the course of this short and introductory treatment.

We must bear in mind first of all, however, that a significant aspect of philosophy lies in examining our questions themselves, lest we should get into difficulties by attempting precipitately to answer misleading, ill-formed, or badly-understood questions. It is for this reason that chapter 1 is devoted to a discussion of the question posed above, and to this we will now turn.

1: asking the right question

We (reflective human beings, I mean) divide things in the world into two categories – those which think, and those which do not. People, and probably monkeys, cats and dogs, think. Bricks and biscuits, and probably plants, on the other hand, do not think. In some cases, such as flies and earthworms, most people are unsure what to say. Thus we seem to have two sets of things, with a somewhat fuzzy no-man's land between them.

This distinction is by no means symmetrical. Firstly, those things which think do not *always* think – for example, they are (most people would accept) without thoughts during much of the time when they are asleep. Things which do not think, however, are without thoughts *all* of the time: there are no lapses into thoughtfulness! The distinction is, then, between those things which *sometimes* think and those which *never* think; between those things which are capable of thought and those which are incapable of it.

Secondly, it is clear that at least some of the things which think are capable of making this very distinction, whilst none of those things which do not think are capable of doing so. We are dealing, therefore, with a distinction imposed from the only side of the divide capable of making distinctions of any sort. Nor could there, even in principle, be any 'objective' arbiter who could make such a distinction from a position of neutrality, since the categories Thinking Being and Non-Thinking Being are obviously jointly exhaustive – everything falls into one and only one of them.

All of this sounds, on the face of it, very straightforward, though, as we shall see, it is not. It is, however, a great deal more straightforward than what comes next. So far, we have noticed that human beings are unhesitatingly regarded as thinking beings, and that as we go through the animal kingdom in what used to be called the direction of 'down', we are increasingly less inclined to ascribe thought to the creatures we encounter. When we reach plants, all but the very unorthodox are certain that no real thinking is going on. And when we come to to inanimate things – those which are not even *alive* – we are all agreed on its absence. Or are we?

There is one special case, which for obvious reasons has only come to serious attention in recent decades. This is the case of the 'intelligent' machine. It has been suggested by quite a lot of more-or-less influential people, that it would be possible to build a computer which not only behaves as a simple tool, like an hour-glass or an abacus, but which *really thinks*, in the sense in which you and I really think. Some have gone further and hinted that certain of our existing machines may have this property. It will be the task of the remainder of this book to examine claims of these kinds. Can computers really think or can't they? And if they can't, could they perhaps if they were only a little more complex? Or a *lot* more? Or could they never do so, however sophisticated we made them? Let us (as befits reflective human beings) reflect.

knowing what we mean

If the question were even as simple as it seems, this book would probably be a great deal shorter. As it is, I am going to begin by playing what many will see as a typical philosopher's trick, and say, 'It depends what you mean by "really think".' Like most such questions, this looks odd at first sight. When someone says, 'Be quiet, I'm thinking', or 'Aunt Ethel is thinking about Iceland again', we stand in need of no clarification regarding the meaning of the word 'thinking'. In our present context, however, a more searching analysis is called for; not so much because these everyday uses are vague or ambiguous, but because the question we are considering is not merely to do with recognizing well-understood central cases of thinking, or even with particular instances at all, but with what we might call the 'essence' of thought. This grand-sounding phrase really only means that we are concerned with what does and does not *count as* thinking. For this reason, it will be useful to attempt some sort of characterization of what we mean by 'really think' when we ask whether a computer could really think. In the rest of this chapter, it is important to remember that we are not merely casting about for a stipulative definition – a question that can be settled by definition is not a philosophical question at all. Rather, we have identified a question which actually arises for some people, and which genuinely puzzles them; and we want to pin down that question, that source of puzzlement, in such a way that we do not end up by offering an answer to the wrong question.

thinking as intelligence

We have already seen that the question of whether machines can think tends to arise in connection with those machines which are described as 'intelligent'. It makes sense, then, to begin by asking whether being capable of thought is the same thing as being, in this sense, intelligent.

Intelligent machines are machines which have (a) a store of residual knowledge, and (b) some sophisticated means of applying it in a given case. This means that the machine in some way incorporates or has access to a data base (a store of facts), and also carries some quite complex software for handling new cases and relating them to what it already 'knows'. Since these are not strictly part of the machine itself, the whole set-up is usually known as an 'intelligent system'. Now is this the type of intelligence which we might want to identify with thought in the fullest sense?

One reason for *not* making this simple equation is the merely quantitative nature of the criterion which we would be applying were we to do so. One thing which impresses people about 'intelligent systems' is the amount of information they can store. A typical data base can hold many thousands of times more facts than any human being could hope to remember. Another is the speed at which they can search through this data and respond to interrogation, and the vast multiplicity of possible responses which they are capable of making. Yet all this differs only in degree from, say, a word processor with a built-in spelling checker. True, we must be wary of writing off enormous differences of complexity as 'mere' differences of degree – the ability of human beings to think no doubt has *something* to do with their degree of complexity. Yet it cannot surely be a matter of just more facts, more combinations of facts, quicker access to facts, and so on: somewhere along the line, the capacity for thought must depend on the *kind* of complexity involved. No sheer degree of capacity or speed can be actually *identified* with real thought. And the same goes even when we take into account some of the more impressive things which such systems can do, such as drawing inferences, or distinguishing between relevant and irrelevant information.

Whilst these 'mechanical' kinds of ability are no doubt *necessary* for genuine thought, it is highly implausible to suggest that they are *sufficient*. That is to say, whilst anything which genuinely thinks must be able to perform to some extent the sort of tricks which an 'intelligent system' can do, it by no means follows that anything which does these tricks is thereby capable of genuine thought. We have to conclude that the concept of thought in the fullest sense cannot be just the same as that of intelligence, in the sense in which machines can be 'intelligent'. This is not, of course, to pre-judge the issue against the view that machines can think: it simply means that the person who suspects that the computer might be 'really thinking' must be being tempted to attribute something extra to it, *over and above* (though possibly arising out of) its sheer capacity and complexity of data-handling.

If real thought were the same thing as this mechanical sort of intelligence, our task would be an easy one: of course some machines are intelligent – they can work out square roots, direct space rockets, and so on – therefore by definition they think. Unfortunately, this too-easy equation falls to bits as soon as we start to prod at it a little, and we will have to look further in order to discover what that 'extra' ingredient referred to above could be.

thinking as creativity

One possible candidate is *creativity*. A promising sign is that this is *par excellence* one of those attributes about which disagreement is rife when it comes to attributing it to machines: some people maintain that no machine could ever exhibit creativity, whilst others tell us that creative machines are already in existence.

The trouble here, of course, is pinning down the meaning of 'creativity' itself. The first trap which we must avoid is that of regarding creativity as exclusively the province of gifted artists, musicians and the like. It may be that the everyday human characteristic of creativity is better developed in such persons, but for our purposes we require nothing very highflown. If creativity is an essential component of genuine thought, then it must be a kind of creativity exemplified, to a greater or lesser extent, by everyone. The sorts of things we will have in mind

Others tell us that creative machines are already in existence.

here are, we might suggest, (a) the ability to come up with new solutions to problems, that is, solutions which are not part of a repertoire which has been explicitly taught to the person or thing in question, and (b) the propensity to initiate interest in some topic or activity without having been overtly directed to it by a controlling agency: in other words, to act with some degree of *autonomy*. This idea of autonomy is very important, and we shall be returning to it in chapter 10. What, then, of these two features?

Certainly a thing which instantiates these characteristics will be a better candidate for 'really thinking' than one which does not. Yet there are drawbacks here also. Take firstly the idea of creativity as the ability to generate new solutions. It will be claimed that there exist machines already which can do this. However, when we look at the way in which they do it, we find that they have, naturally, been programmed to do so, and to do so by carrying out a predetermined, mechanical, procedure. And we have already noted, in the last section, that such 'mechanical' abilities, whilst they might in some way *support* real thinking, cannot be *identified* with it. The ability to generate original solutions does not, then, seem to have brought with it what we were looking for – the characteristic or ingredient which makes the difference between mere data-juggling and genuine thought.

And if we take the second feature which we associated with creativity – the ability to initiate interest in something – we will find that it gets us little further. Suppose we have a system which is somehow so advanced that when I instruct it to play a game of chess with me it sometimes says, 'No, I'm getting more interested in bridge just at the moment'. How did it arrive at this response? Surely there are only two possibilities: either that was the only thing it *could* have done, because it was programmed to do that, or it was totally mysterious how it arrived at the answer. But worse is to come. For if we accept this, why should we accept anything different when it comes to human beings? If a friend gives me the same response, how do we explain how *he* arrived at it? Of course, it is not utterly mysterious to us how other people come to have the interests which they do – in a sense, we know quite a lot about it. We commonly explain this sort of thing by reference to such factors as the choices available to a person at a given time, the extent of that person's knowledge, the current influences on him, and so on. And in the case of explaining the interests of a *person*, we would refer to *reasons* as well as *causes*: that is, we would regard some of the relevant antecedents as things which may have been taken into rational consideration by the person in question, as opposed to forces acting 'blindly' on him. The trouble is that the 'ingredient' of human beings which makes it appropriate to ascribe reasons as well as causes to them, is itself something of a philosophical puzzle: we find ourselves unsure of what it is, even in ourselves, which distinguishes authentic 'creativity' in this sense from some purely mechanical process. We will return to this topic later. It is enough here to recognise that the difference between simply obeying a 'program' and being truly creative, is proving as hard to nail down as the original distinction between 'real' and merely 'apparent' thought, which it was meant to illuminate.

creatures with minds

This is perhaps the appropriate point at which to try out a more general concept, and one with a very long history. This is the idea of 'the mind', as opposed to the purely physical aspect or component of a thing. One way, at least, of registering the fact that human beings actually *think* is to say that besides or because of, or as a feature of the kind of physical make-up which we have, we can also be said to have *minds*. We found in the last section that the notion of creativity raised at least as many problems as it was meant to solve, and it will almost certainly turn out to be the same with the concept of the mind. However, it will be found worthwhile going into this approach, since it does appear to bring us closer to what people commonly think of when they attempt to articulate what it is that characterizes thinking beings as opposed to those with merely mechanical or calculative abilities. The problems raised by the idea of having a 'mind' will be tackled in more detail in a later chapter, when we come to look at the variety of existing approaches to this subject. It will be sufficient at this stage to introduce a further concept, which has normally been taken as central to the idea of 'the mind'. This is the notion of *consciousness*, which will be of cardinal importance to much of what follows in this book.

thinking as consciousness

When we ask whether or not a thing – an organism or machine or whatever – is conscious, we are asking much more than whether it is able to carry out this or that task, however 'clever' or complex the task may be. What we are asking is: *does it have a point of view?* Or, to express the same thing another way: *does it have an 'inside' as well as an 'outside'?* Some people may find no oddity at all in this question. Others may find it hoplessly abstract and, in the most ominous sense of the word, 'philosophical'. Let us try to sharpen it up a little.

One reason for not believing that a brick can think, is that the question 'What would it be like to be a brick?' strikes us as making very little sense. It isn't just that we have no way of telling what the experience of bricks is like; if we thought that bricks had experiences we could always say something like, 'Well, people get hold of you and cement you to walls'. Rather, we are not inclined to think that being a brick is like anything at all, for we are not tempted to believe that bricks have experiences of any kind. It is in this sense that a brick presents itself to us as something with an 'outside' but no 'inside': something which has no viewpoint of its own on the world, although some things in the world, of course, have a viewpoint on *it*. To put it as its crudest and also, perhaps, its vaguest, we do not feel, in considering the brick, that there is 'anyone at home' there.

We noticed earlier in this chapter that those things which think nevertheless do not think *all* of the time, whilst non-thinking things *never* think. We may now make the point that a *conscious* being is one which has that feature which you and I have when we are awake, but lack when we are asleep. Conscious beings (beings capable of consciousness) are not necessarily always conscious, whilst the other sort never are.

It is probably the concept of consciousness above all, which is at the bottom of the distinction between 'real' or 'genuine' thought, and that kind of intelligence, or whatever, of which some machines are obviously capable. A creature which actually thinks is one which 'knows what it is doing', in the richest possible sense of 'knows'. It is one which has its own point of view – or, if we like, has 'its own world'; one which is not just an extension of its creator, designer or programmer.

When we have said this, it must by no means be thought that our problems in this direction are over. On the contrary, they are only just beginning; for we have so far done little more than gesture at the idea which we are trying to capture. However, it does seem as though we have arrived at a workable approach to what people have in mind when they wonder whether a computer might be 'really thinking'. It is chiefly to this idea which we shall be addressing ourselves in subsequent chapters.

some apparent confusions

Unfortunately, things are not so straightforward as might appear from the foregoing. For the ideas of 'genuine thought' and 'consciousness' do not by any means refer to just the same thing. There is, for example, good reason for believing that many of the lower animals are conscious, in the sense that they have sensations, see and hear, feel pain, heat and cold and so on: yet we would certainly hesitate before calling what they do 'thinking'. Thinking suggests the kind of abilities to form concepts, to make judgements, and to reason, which such creatures clearly lack. On the other hand (and more dubiously), some people are inclined to attribute thought in the absence of consciousness, especially in the case of machines: one hears it said, for example, that the question of whether machines can think does not depend on whether or not they have conscious mental states. It is true that psychologists often talk of activities which we would normally call thinking, as taking place sub-consciously, or even unconsciously. However, a significant difference between unconscious thought on the part of human beings, and the non-conscious 'thinking' of machines, is that human beings are *sometimes* conscious; and the possibility of unconscious thinking seems to depend on the existence of at least some conscious experience.

To avoid these apparent confusions and to capture what is intended to be our topic, we shall speak of 'conscious thought' as referring to the intersection of the two features – that is, those cases which are both cases of consciousness and of thinking. Later on, in chapter 10, some arguments will be presented to the effect that there is in fact a fairly tight logical connection between the two things. For now, however, we will move on to look at the notion of consciousness in more detail, and also, in the process, to uncover a further obstacle to our enquiry.

2: symptoms of consciousness

So far, we have done no more than to formulate a rather loose idea of what it is that we are asking when we ask if a machine can, or could, *really* think. We have still gone no way towards giving an answer to the question thus formulated. It is to this task that we now turn.

How, then, can we begin to tell whether a given machine, or a machine of a given type and degree of complexity, is conscious? How, for that matter, can we tell in general whether anything is conscious or not? It will be best to begin by discussing human beings, since we are, presumably, more certain that they are sometimes conscious than we are in the case of other things around us.

how to tell whether someone is conscious

On the face of it, it's fairly simple to discover whether a person is conscious at a given time or not. When people are conscious, they tend to move, talk, and respond to external stimuli such as kicks, pricks, pinches and punches. When people are *un*conscious, they tend to remain stationary and relatively quiet, they don't respond, at least in the normal way, to external stimuli, they fall over when forcibly propped against walls, and so on. We can only say 'tend to' since there are grey areas like sleepwalking or daydreaming. But these do not alter the fact that there are many cases in which no doubt is involved, and some symptoms of consciousness which are overwhelmingly reliable. In no sense are we always, or even often, in the dark about whether a human being is conscious.

16

But let us now ask: what status does this certainty have? At this point, we must remind ourselves of an important distinction between two ways in which the word 'certain' is used. In one way of using it, the certainty lies in the mind of the person who is certain of the thing in question. For example, I am certain that I have a pipe in my jacket pocket, though I recognize that it is *possible* that I am mistaken. My turning out to be mistaken would not convince me that I had not really been certain of it at all. In the other way of using it, the certainty lies in the fact itself: it is certain because it *could not be otherwise*. For example, we may say that it is certain that animals which eat meat are carnivores. This is not equivalent to saying that this or that person, or even everybody, is 'certain in their mind' that this is the case. What is meant is, rather, that it is certain in the sense that it is *logically* true: once we know that something eats meat, it follows without any possible doubt that it is carnivorous. It is not like the certainty of the whereabouts of my pipe, since once I recognize the connection, in this latter case, I cannot entertain the possibility that it might turn out to be otherwise, for to suppose this will make no sense. Also, unlike the 'certain in the mind' use of 'certain', if it turns out that I *have* somehow made a mistake, for example about the meanings of the words, then I have to accept, not just that it is not the case, but that there never was any certainty of this kind about it at all.

Now in which sense are we certain, at least in the clearest, most central cases, that if people talk, respond, move about without bumping into things etc., then they are in fact conscious? It seems that it cannot be the latter, stronger, sense, since it is *possible* (i.e. involves no contradiction) to imagine just such physical creatures which do all these things and yet are not conscious, have no point of view on the world, have an 'outside' but no 'inside'. We can imagine, in other words, all these kinds of behaviour being exhibited without there being 'anybody at home'.

But if we must accept that our certainty that other people are conscious is only a matter of being 'certain in our own minds', then there is a logical gap between the premise (the fact that such behaviour is exhibited) and the conclusion (that consciousness is present). And if there is such a gap between the evidence and what it is evidence for, then, it may be argued, there is room for doubt. And if there is room for doubt, then surely we must not regard as totally unreasonable, a person who seriously thinks there are no other minds in the world than his own – who really believes that other people are merely automata whose characteristics are exhausted by the physical aspect they present, or could present, to him. A person who takes this view is called a *solipsist*. It might be worth issuing a warning here that there are more and less sophisticated types of solipsism, and that what has been outlined above is only a very crude form.

Of course, *how* reasonable we think the solipsist's position to be must depend on how good we think the evidence is for the consciousness of other people. If we think that the evidence is, under the circumstances, quite poor, then the solipsist's conclusion will present a genuine threat; but if we believe the evidence to be still pretty sound, then the solipsist will emerge as a person obstinately embracing a position for no better reason than that it can't be shown to be false (and perhaps also that it appeals to him). Yet this doesn't somehow seem good enough. Is there not something wrong with the position which we have got ourselves into, of having to take seriously *at all* the idea that even other people, let alone computers, don't really think? Before exploring what might have gone wrong, we will look at an even stronger argument for the solipsist, to the effect that the 'evidence' for other people's consciousness is not just inconclusive, but is really no evidence at all. But first, let us return for a moment to our central topic, the relation between computers and thought.

machines aren't like people
Another thing which might be troubling us in the above discussion of the evidence for human consciousness, is that it seems to suggest a misleading model for the evidence of machine consciousness. For it appears to suggest that the way to tell whether a machine is conscious is to watch it and see

whether it jumps around, responds to stimuli and so on. Two things must make us wary of this approach. The first is that many of the kinds of machines to which people are tempted to attribute consciousness do *not* do these things. The sorts of machine which do move around in a vaguely human-like way tend largely to be ones like manufacturing robots which, far from being capable of independent thought, are typically designed for a simple task such as screwing nuts on to bolts, and go haywire in a very 'thing-like' way when faced with a comparatively trivial difficulty such as being given a washer instead of a nut. On the other hand, the 'intelligent' machines which some suspect of real thought are usually ones which just sit there receiving data and giving answers. Only if the producing of text on a screen can be counted as fully 'responding' can such machines be said to respond in the same sense that people do.

Secondly, building a machine which simulates at least *some* of the things a human person can do like moving about, saying 'good morning' and so on, is not difficult at all. In short, (i) it doesn't seem that a machine has to be animate in order for it to come under suspicion of doing some genuine thinking, and (ii) it *does* seem, at least superficially, that almost any fool can build a machine which is in some sense animate, though no one would suspect *it* of conscious thought simply on account of its animation. All this clearly raises problems in the light of what has been said earlier in this chapter about everyday 'symptoms of consciousness'. We will come back to these problems in a later chapter. First, however, let us look at the stronger argument for solipsism mentioned above – an argument which also casts doubts on the relevance of the argument from everyday symptoms as evidence of consciousness.

the solipsist's (apparent) trump card
The trump card which the solipsist is able to play lies in the following consideration. Although we have so far proceeded on the assumption that certain things count as evidence of a sort for consciousness in others, it can easily be argued that the onus is squarely on the believer in other minds to show how

this 'evidence' can be evidence at all, let alone conclusive or even persuasive evidence. For the stubborn fact which the solipsist is always able to fall back on, is that there is no demonstrable connection between the kind of 'symptoms' in question, and the presence of real mentality. Whereas in some other contexts we can argue the presence of B from that of A on the basis of their having appeared in conjunction in all, or most, known instances, the case of other minds is different in that there are no available manifest instances of such a conjunction, since other minds by their nature cannot be directly accessible. The only conscious thought to which any given person has first hand access, is his own. And to argue from the fact that the 'symptoms' are accompanied by genuine mentality in oneself, to the conclusion that the same symptoms are likely to be accompanied by it in others, seems, at first sight, to be a very weak sort of argument indeed, since it draws a conclusion about a whole great class of instances on the basis of a consideration of only one of them! This point will be discussed in the next chapter, when we come to deal explicitly with the 'Argument from Analogy' for other minds. The problem to bear in mind here is that an upholder of the solipsistic position can, it seems, put the ball in his opponent's court by simply pointing to the fact that mental states are private (which is undoubtedly true). If it seems that this argument is too crude to do the job for which it is intended, let us be patient and attend to what follows.

It appears that what we lack is certainly not *prima facie* evidence but, as it were, evidence that this *prima facie* evidence is indeed evidence at all; that is, a justification for treating these very obvious 'symptoms' as symptoms of anything in the first place. This, then, is the result, for our present discussion, of the fact that mental states are essentially private. It must not be thought, from the above, that the reader is being invited to entertain seriously the solipsist position. Indeed, someone who seriously did adopt it would in fact be a psychopath rather than a philosopher (though Bertrand Russell is said to have received a letter from a lady who affirmed that she was a convinced solipsist, and could not understand why everybody else wasn't!). However, the real philosophical issue is not so much an open-ended enquiry into the question of whether other people have minds or not, as a puzzle concerning what can have gone wrong for us to find ourselves in this position in the first place. If solipsism is, in practice, untenable, then the arguments which seem to place the onus on the critic of it must have been in some way invalid or misleading in the first place. We will move on, in the next chapter, to look at some of the philosophical positions which have been adopted in response to this difficulty, which in modern philosophy goes under the name of the 'Problem of Other Minds'.

3: the problem of other minds

We now seem to have reasoned ourselves into an even more absurd position than previously. For it appears not just that there is room for the sceptic about other minds to hold his position if he wishes to, but that the onus is on the *believer* in other minds to show that there is anything in his favour at all! In order, then, to get our discussion into logical order, we must tackle head-on the question of how other-minds scepticism can be answered. That is, before deciding whether to attribute minds to things other than human beings, we must be sure that we know that we can, and *why* we can, attribute minds even to other human beings.

We will begin by looking at the views of a modern writer, Richard Rorty, who presents us with a good starting point since he argues, in effect, that there is, or need be, no problem of other minds at all. If we can go along with all that Rorty says, it will obviously save us a lot of unnecessary trouble.

Rorty's rejection of the 'mirror of nature'
Among Rorty's avowed aims in his writing on this topic are 'to undermine the reader's confidence in "the mind" as something about which there ought to be a "theory"'. It is only to be expected, then, that he himself does not have a theory about our knowledge of other minds, in the sense that many other philosophers have had. Assuming that we already have some confidence to undermine, let us see how Rorty goes about attempting to do this.

Central to Rorty's position is the idea that much of the

traditional Western philosophy of mind rests on, not exactly a mistake, but on philosophers' having been under the spell of a particular set of pictures, or metaphors, concerning our mental life. The chief among these is the idea of man as having a 'glassy essence' (a phrase coined by Shakespeare), of possessing a mind which is the 'mirror of nature'. To unpack the metaphors a bit, this means it has traditionally been regarded as characteristic of man that he is capable of mental states which are at least sometimes like 'reflections' of things in the physical world – for every physical thing of which I am aware, there is a sort of mental counterpart in me, existing in a 'non-material medium'. These are not, however, on the traditional view, the only contents of the mind: there are also such things as beliefs, desires, intentions, and 'raw feels' (such as pains, and uninterpreted sensations such as young babies have). Of these, it is perhaps the 'raw feels' which are the hardest to have doubts about, since it is with these that we are most immediately acquainted.

This immediacy of acquaintance with at least some of the contents of our minds is, Rorty argues, partly what lies at the bottom of the confusion which he sees in traditional philosophy of mind. For according to him, it results in a temptation to 'deduce' from the fact that we know our own minds better than anything else, that we could still know the contents of our own minds even if we knew *nothing* else (i.e. that things could still be the same in our minds even if the solipsist were correct). And further, to draw the conclusion that knowing whether something has a mind involves knowing it *as well as it knows itself*. If this latter is true, then it is easy to see how total other-minds scepticism results. For, in this sense, I *cannot* know another person as well as that person knows himself, since I cannot have his experiences.

why I can't have your experiences
Here, let us interrupt the discussion of Rorty for a moment, to get something clear. Some may doubt, at first, the impossibility of having someone else's experiences. If so, then ask what would *count as* having the experiences of another person.

Clearly it cannot just be a matter of seeing, hearing, touching, the same *things*: for although there may be a single flower which is the flower that you and I are both looking at, there are undoubtedly *two* experiences (however qualitatively similar) of the flower – yours and mine. Suppose, though, that only you were actually seeing the flower, but that my brain was somehow wired up to yours in such a way that the experience was transmitted 'directly' from your brain to mine. Would I then be having *your* experience? We must still say that I wouldn't, since it remains possible to talk about 'my' experience of the episode and 'your' experience of it; and, as a result, to doubt whether they are in fact qualitatively identical. The fact that such doubt could occur is sufficient to show that there is no strict identity between your experience and mine. If we had actual identity (i.e. one thing and not two) no question could arise about how far A is similar to B, provided we understood them properly, since 'A' and 'B' would be just two ways of referring to the same thing. The reason why I can never have your experience is, at bottom, a *logical* one: if we *both* experience something, then there are two experiences of it and not one. Only if we were one person and not two people, would it count as one experience and not two – but then nobody would be having the experience of *another* person!

self-knowledge as observation

To return to Rorty's argument, he rejects the piece of reasoning which seems to lead to the (impossible) requirement that we must know something as well as it knows itself – i.e. 'from the inside' – if we are to know whether it has a mind or not. (Of course, it will only *have* an inside if it has a mind, since the two things are the same.) The apparent plausibility of the reasoning is, he believes, a result of the model (which he attributes to Descartes) of self-knowledge as akin to *observation*. What does this mean?

Consider what happens when someone, let's say, asks you whether you have a headache, and that you reply sincerely, 'Yes'. Was any *observation* going on prior to your answering? Did you have the feeling of spying on some secret realm known only to yourself and concealed from everyone else? Rorty would want to say something like the following. It's certainly true that nobody else could have answered the question with the certainty that you could. But doesn't the very immediacy of the experience itself rule out the idea that you needed to make an observation in order to answer the question? Surely the headache wasn't something which you *came to know* by self-observation ('introspection', as philosophers sometimes call it) and subsequently *reported*, but something which you simply *had*, and just *expressed* faithfully by your answer much as the young child expresses the same thing by crying, only in a more sophisticated and conventional fashion. In fact, Rorty goes further than this, and says that 'the way in which the pre-linguistic infant knows that it has a pain is the way in which the record-changer knows the spindle is empty'. This is undoubtedly controversial, since people have usually considered that an infant, however pre-linguistic, has 'feels' in a way which the record-changer does not. Equally clearly, this has important implications for our own concern with the relation between the 'minds' of people and the 'minds' of machines.

Rorty and the aliens
In connection with this, Rorty asks us to consider a hypothetical race of people on another planet, who don't possess the concept of a mental state at all. They use words corresponding to 'believe', 'intend' and the like, though they don't know what is meant by calling these 'states of mind'. On the other hand, they do not have the concepts of 'idea', 'perception', or 'mental representation'. In other words, all those mentalistic concepts which refer to what 'represents' or 'mirrors' things in the world, and can be *immediately present* to the person who has them, are unknown to them. Furthermore, he asks us to suppose that these people, instead of talking about mental states, talk only of *neurological states* (since neurology and biochemistry are what they are best at). Thus, when a child is in danger of burning itself, on that planet, the mother will say, 'Be careful – you'll stimulate your C-fibres!' (the neurological state corresponding to being in pain).

Now we are invited to speculate on what will happen when a group of philosophers from Earth try to discover whether these people actually have minds or not, whether they are 'really' conscious. This they take to be equivalent to, or to depend crucially on, the question: do they have sensations, or 'raw feels' (the most basic mental item) or not? The next point is of great importance, and shows us why 'raw feels' are what the mentalist philosopher most wants to insist on. It is that our knowledge (if that is what it is) of these items is *incorrigible*. Take the case of pain. The distinctive thing about a sensation such as a pain, is that I cannot be in any doubt whether I am having it or not. For it to *seem* to me as if I were in pain would be the same as *being* in pain, as is brought out ironically in the well-worn limerick:

> There was a faith-healer from Beale
> Who said 'Although pain isn't real,
> When I sit on a pin
> And it punctures my skin,
> I dislike what I *fancy* I feel!'

Now what will our aliens say about all this? Suppose they know of a neural state, which they call state T-435, that corresponds to its *seeming as though* the C-fibres are stimulated (i.e. as though one were in the neural state associated with pain); suppose further, that sometimes one of them is in state T-435 though it turns out that his C-fibres are not stimulated. From this it will be clear that it is possible for these people to be mistaken about whether they are in the neural state corresponding to pain. We can then ask if they can be wrong about whether they are in a neural state T-435, and once again they might say, 'Yes, it sometimes happens'. Thus they can even be wrong about whether they are in the neural state associated with the seeming-to-be-in-the-pain-type-state. The point is that none of this is going to tell us whether or not they have sensations ('raw feels') about which they *cannot* be wrong. Nothing at all that we can discover about them seems to be relevant to whether these raw feels are present – and furthermore, they themselves do not, we will remember, possess the concepts of such feels and sensations at all. The feels and sensations just seem to drop out of the question altogether.

This gets us back to Rorty's rejection of the idea of a mental world accessible only to the person whose world it is. The aliens can't *tell* us anything relevant to deciding whether or not they have a mental life, so if we still want to ask the question, we must be talking about something which is, in principle, *incommunicable*. But if the fact that someone really is, for example, in pain (has the raw feel, and not just the outward behaviour) is incommunicable to others, then it can have nothing to do with the use of the *word* 'pain' or what it means. For our language concerning sensations, pains and so on, is clearly a means of communication, and anything which it might be *about* is of course communicable. Thus, whatever we are talking about, in talking about 'raw feels' or 'sensations', it seems that it cannot be what is referred to by what we regard as our sensation vocabularly ('pain', 'feeling' etc.)! In making this kind of point, Rorty is influenced by the earlier twentieth-century philosopher Wittgenstein, some of whose views we will be considering later. Rorty concludes that scepticism about other minds is, properly understood, philosophically uninteresting, in much the same way as scepticism about the external world is (he says) uninteresting. We cannot *know* or *prove* that tables and chairs exist when they are not being observed, but what we do know is that, if they don't, their absence makes no difference to anything. Nothing depends on it, for a world in which they don't is, for *all* purposes, the same as a world in which they do; and much the same is true, Rorty suggests, of other minds.

Not surprisingly, many people do not accept this view, and would rather stick firmly to the idea that other minds do make a difference, and that other-minds scepticism needs to be met head-on rather than (as they see it) brushed under the carpet. Before looking at an example of the head-on approach, we will briefly consider a view of other minds which is in some ways like, and in other ways unlike, Rorty's.

consciousness as a status

Rorty, whilst arguing that the 'problem of other minds' is no longer philosophically interesting once its origins are understood properly, still accepts the existence, in some sense, of states of consciousness which are irreducibly mental. Some philosophers, however, have taken a slightly different tack (which Rorty himself could easily have taken but does not), and maintained that genuine thought, or consciousness, is more like a *status* which we *ascribe* to another person than a property which they actually independently possess.

In order to make clearer what is meant here by 'ascribing a status', let us look first of all at a three-way distinction which has been made by the present-day American philosopher Daniel Dennett. He talks of three possible 'stances' which we might take in dealing with some object such as a machine. These are, firstly the *physical stance*, secondly the *design stance*, and lastly the *intentional stance*. Note that 'intentional' here is a bit of philosophers' jargon, and does not mean what we mean by it in ordinary language. The concept of 'intentionality' was largely developed by the philosophers Franz Brentano (1838-1917) and Edmund Husserl (1859-1938). It refers to the feature of 'directedness', or 'having an object', i.e. being *about* something, which they regarded as the characteristic mark of conscious thought.

What, then, do these three stances involve? Suppose you want to explain *why* some machine does a particular thing which it does. Take first of all a simple machine like a catapault, and ask why the stone gets thrown at a given time. The explanation which we would all give is a purely physical one such as, 'The lever gets thrust forward by a sudden release of the torsion on a bow of coiled rope, and stopped by a wooden butt, thus releasing the missile'. Now take a more complex kind of device, like a modern washing machine. Why, we may ask, does it empty itself part way through the cycle and pour fresh water over the contents? Here, we will not be likely to give an explanation in terms of purely mechanical workings of the machine, but rather in terms of the purposes of the designer. We will say something like, 'It's meant to rinse the clothes and wash the soap away'. Here, we have passed from the physical stance, which is what we adopted in the case of the catapult, to the design stance. The characteristic thing about the design stance is that, although we refer not to the physical make-up of the machine, but to some motives, intentions, purposes etc. (i.e. mental kinds of things), they are not ascribed to the machine itself, but to the person who designed it.

Now thirdly, take an even more sophisticated machine, such as a chess-playing machine. What kind of reply do we give when asked a question like 'Why did it retract that knight?'? The chances are that the explanation we give will be neither in terms of mechanics nor of design. The internal workings of the machine and the details of the chess-playing software will be too complex for almost anyone to hold in their head thoroughly enough to explain the knight's move by reference to them. Furthermore, an explanation involving the designer's purposes will be almost as hard to give. The exact way in which the general strategy which the programmer intended the software to embody, such as to avoid loss of pieces or to try to gain control of the centre of the board, connects with the fact that this particular move was made at this point in the game, is probably so remote and tortuous that it is opaque even to the programmer herself. The way we will almost certainly go about explaining it is to talk as though this machine (or this program, or this-machine-in-the-control-of-this-program) has purposes *of its own*. That is, we will say something like, 'It doesn't want to risk losing the knight to your king's rook', or 'It's trying to block your queen's advance'. Of course we won't, deep down, regard the machine as actually thinking. We know, at the back of our mind, that behind the intentional-type behaviour of the machine lies a design, and behind the design lie some 'brute' physical facts about its make-up. In other words, we know that it would be possible *in principle* to give an explanation in more fundamental terms than we do; it is just simpler and more natural to describe the behaviour of so sophisticated a machine in mentalistic language.

the circularity of the 'status' view

It is this very consideration, however, which has led some philosophers to wonder whether the same might not be true of the way in which we use mental concepts when talking about each other. (Here we must not include Dennett, whose own views are considerably less simple.) The idea is that there is no 'fact of the matter' about whether other people are conscious. This claim can be supported, if necessary, by some of the considerations we saw in looking at Rorty. Rather, we simply cannot avoid taking a mentalistic, intentional stance towards them, since the details of their physical make-up are, despite Rorty's aliens, far too complex to refer to all the time, and we don't regard them as being designed for a purpose in the sense that machines are. This view has a good deal of initial appeal, since it simplifies the world in the kind of way a good theory should. Both people and machines are 'really' just physical things, and all their actions are *in principle* capable of explanation on the purely physical level. But when a thing gets too sophisticated to handle by reference to physics, or the purposes of a designer, we respond to it by the use of mentalistic concepts.

Unfortunately, or perhaps fortunately, things are not so straightforward. How, we may ask, can this view explain the fact that anything can *ascribe* consciousness to anything else, or take up any stance *towards* it? Remember that in the case of the machine we are supposed to bear in mind that it's not *really* thinking – we just talk *as though* it were. Now if human beings are in some sense in the same position, then who is doing the ascribing? Who is it that is genuinely taking up a stance towards something else? The answer seems to be 'No one'. For if intentionality, that is the capacity to think about something, is not an independent property a thing has, but always, even in the case of human beings, only a concept which *others* use about *it*, then the situation seems to be as follows. Not only will the capacity for 'real thought' be ascribed rather than independently existing, but the *ability to ascribe thought* will itself be only ascribed. But this is surely circular. No one can be the first to acquire the feature in question, for possessing the feature depends on having it attributed by someone who already has it.

Rather than pursue this point further, we will now go on to look at a view which is far removed from those we have seen so far in this chapter. It comes from the philosopher Thomas Nagel, and may serve to sharpen up some of our reservations about the theses described above.

Nagel and the bats

Thomas Nagel, although a well-known writer in various areas of philosophy, is probably best known for his famous question 'What is it like to be a bat?', the title of an essay in which it occurs. The important thing is not so much answering the question, as noticing that it makes sense to ask it. Nagel chooses bats for the example since they are high enough up the evolutionary tree for us to have little doubt that they have conscious experience and yet at the same time their activities are sufficiently different from ours to make them distinctly alien to us. The point of the question 'What is it like to be a bat?' is that, in Nagel's view, the essence of our belief that bats have experience is that *there is something that it is like to be a bat*. More generally, he says 'the fact that an organism has conscious experience...means, basically, that there is something it is like to *be* that organism'. What he has done here is to give some substantive content to the abstractions which we have discussed so far, such as 'consciousness' and 'experience'. To say that there is something it is like to be a particular thing, also gives us more to go on, philosophically, than the metaphors with which this topic was introduced in the first chapter, such as having 'an inside as well as an outside', or there being 'someone at home'.

Even more importantly, what Nagel seems to have done by posing the question in this way, is to give us a new starting point in the problem of other minds, by providing a means of expressing what it is that we are saying about other creatures when we attribute minds, or consciousness, to them. A means, also, which seems to be free of the drawbacks which afflict talk of 'sensations', 'feels' and so on. For in the case of these latter, all that could count as evidence in favour of their presence, seems nevertheless to be consistent with their absence. And this includes any avowals which a person might make, of having conscious experience: the words 'I am really in pain' are just a piece of behaviour like any other, and the pain *itself* drops out of the picture through sheer incommunicability.

How does Nagel's approach help us here? Well, unlike saying that a thing has sensations or feels, saying that there is 'something it is like' to be that thing is to make a statement which could not be true unless its internal, shadowy counterpart really did exist. We saw that words like 'pain' and 'sensation' could operate just as they do, in the absence of the 'raw feels' to which we are tempted to think that they refer. Nagel's formulation is not like this; indeed, it could have no meaning at all unless there were some way in which it can at least sometimes have an answer. To explain this a little more: there is no way in which Nagel's question can still have meaning, if our mental vocabulary is really only about outward behaviour, and not about 'internal' states. And it *does* seem to us that the question makes sense.

However, as many philosophers will be glad to remind us, the fact that a form of words *seems* to have a sense, is no guarantee that it does. Might not this apparently straight-forward question in fact be a piece of disguised nonsense produced by misguided philosophical speculation? For all that has been said so far, it might. For if the 'raw feels' of experience are somehow incommunicable, then it may turn out to be, strictly speaking, a piece of nonsense, on the grounds that to speak of what is incommunicable is nonsensical. But the significant thing about Nagel's formulation is not that it guaran-tees its own meaningfulness (Nagel simply *assumes* that we know what it means alright – and we feel that we do), but that it encapsulates what it is that we want to ask about other creatures, without the possibility of the question itself being 'defused' by the anti-mentalist through being construed in some apparently harmless way. Nagel does, however, make a remark which points us in the direction of a defence of the question as a real and meaningful one. To understand the following, we must bear in mind that the word 'phenomenological' means something like 'how an experience feels *to the person experiencing it*', or maybe rather 'the experience *as it feels to* the person experiencing it'. Nagel says:

> There is a sense in which phenomenological facts are perfectly objective: one person can know or say of another what the quality of the other's experience is. They are subjective, however, in the sense that even this objective ascription of experience is possible only for someone sufficiently similar to the object of the ascription to be able to adopt this point of view – to understand the ascription in the first person as well as in the third, so to speak.

How is being 'sufficiently similar' to a creature supposed to help us in knowing what the quality of that creature's experience is? How can it even help us in knowing that the creature has experiences at all, unless we mean by it 'similar in having the same sort of experiences'? And even then there would be a problem about how we *know* this. To find any answers in this direction, we must go far beyond any mere reformulation of the question, however helpful. And the obvious place to begin is with the 'argument from analogy' which was mentioned in the last chapter.

Russell and the argument from analogy

We saw that the solipsist appears to hold a trump card which he is always able to play against non-solipsists. This is the fact that none of us have, or can have, *direct* evidence for the existence of other minds. However physically like us other people may be, however psychologically plausible their behaviour, there always exists the logical possibility that they are no more than mindless automata. And worse still, if no *direct* evidence exists, it seems that *all* the evidence is rendered worthless, giving us apparently *no* reason to believe in other minds at all.

The argument which these considerations are meant to counter is the 'argument from analogy'; that is, in outline, the argument that people who are like me in *some* respects are probably like me also in possessing consciousness – that the external likeness gives me reason to think that there is 'something it is like to be' them, just as there is something it is like to be me. We will examine briefly two formulations of the argument, one by Bertrand Russell, and the other (a defence of the argument against certain criticisms) by A.J. Ayer.

To take Russell first, he begins by considering the simplest kind of argument from analogy, and showing why it will not hold water. The simplest form is as follows. I know that, for example, when I jump around and rub my foot, it is because of a sensation of pain which I feel in that foot. I therefore conclude that when other people jump around similarly, it is because they have a pain in their foot – a genuine sensation – also. This I do on the grounds that *like causes produce like effects*. What is wrong with this argument as it stands is, Russell points out, that we need to assume, not only that if A causes B on one occasion then A will always cause B, but also that *only* A ever causes B. In other words, we must (illicitly) suppose that if a pain in the foot causes behaviour of a certain kind in me, then whenever behaviour of that kind occurs, it is produced by the same cause – a pain in the foot. But to argue in this way is to neglect the fact that the same behaviour in another person may be caused by a different sensation or by something which is not a sensation at all (i.e. there is no conscious experience of any kind occurring).

To get over this, we need some justification for the above assumption. This Russell finds in the *complexity* of human responses. When an event is of a simple kind like, for example, a loud bang, it is usually the case that it could have been caused in a number of different ways: an explosion, someone dropping a heavy object, a clap of thunder, and so on. But the more complex the event, Russell argues, the less likely it is that it will be subject to multiple causes, since every detail of it will be a result of some particular feature of the cause. Russell sums up his version of the argument from analogy as follows:

> From subjective observation I know that A, which is a thought or feeling, causes B, which is a bodily act, e.g. a statement. I know also that, whenever B is an act of my own body, A is its cause. I now observe an act of the kind B in a body not my own,

and I am having no thought or feeling of the kind A. But I still believe, on the basis of self-observation, that only A can cause B; I therefore infer that there was an A which caused B, though it was not an A that I could observe. On this ground I infer that other people's bodies are associated with minds, which resemble mine in proportion as their bodily behaviour resembles my own.

Will the argument, as formulated by Russell, work? We may notice several things in it to which critics would take exception, such as the notion of 'self-observation' and the idea that one *mind* can 'resemble' another to a measurable degree. For the moment, however, we will pick on one particular line of objection to it. Although Russell seems to have shored up the argument from analogy against the objection from multiple causes, he seems to have done nothing to allay the suspicions of those who attach importance to the fact that we can never have *direct* experience of other people's thoughts, feelings etc. which could reassure us that we are on the right lines in the *indirect* (i.e. analogical) cases. For an attempt at overcoming this obstacle, we must turn to Ayer.

Ayer's defence of the analogy argument

Now Ayer clearly recognizes that there is a case to answer against the sceptic who argues from the above position. And he equally recognizes the nature of the challenge: how can an argument from analogy work, when the conclusion is of a kind which can *never* be *directly* substantiated? In the case of a more usual type of argument from analogy, this is not so. For example, I see shadows on the blind, and infer that there are people in the room, on the grounds that this connection has always been observed to hold in the past. The difference is that I can, if I wish, go into the room and check whether the inference was correct; indeed I probably have done so in the past, and this is what gives me the right to argue from past cases to the present one. But in the case of other minds, there is no such thing as checking whether the analogy holds or not: I cannot argue from the fact that two things are externally alike *plus the fact that the external likeness has been observed to go along with a further likeness in the past*, but only from the fact that the two things are externally alike. How, then, are we justified in assuming that the required analogy, from external likeness to 'inner' likeness, holds at all?

Ayer's response to this is subtle. He begins by comparing the apparent handicap of being logically denied access to another's mental states, with other similar handicaps. For example, I cannot logically have direct access to facts about the past. Nor can I check directly on facts about any region of space where I do not happen to be, since I cannot be both here and somewhere else at the same time. Once we start making these comparisions we are, Ayer thinks, perhaps less tempted to consider that there is something uniquely mysterious about other *minds* as opposed to other times or places which prevents us from knowing *anything* about them. We do not normally think that there is a 'problem of other places', so why should we be worried about the supposed 'problem of other minds'?

But is this argument not too simple? Surely there is a difference between the sense in which I cannot be *somewhere* else, and that in which I cannot be *somebody* else. For the former seems to be merely a physical constraint (I could have been somewhere else if I had wanted to be), whereas the latter is a *logical* contraint (I could not be *someone* else however much I wanted to be).

Ayer has an answer to this, which will be paraphrased rather than reproduced in detail here. Take first of all the idea that I could possibly be somewhere other than where I am. In one sense it is patently false, for no one can be in more than one place at once – the statement 'I am somewhere else' (i.e. somewhere other than where I am) cannot be true when said by anyone, in the same way that the statement, 'I am here' is always true whoever says it. In another sense, however, it is obviously correct, since it is by no means impossible that I should have been at this moment in Brussels, or Leeds, or Istambul, rather than where I happen to be. Now doesn't the same hold for the idea that I could be *somebody* else? For whilst 'I am somebody else' (i.e. somebody other than the person I am) simply cannot be true, the statement 'I am Joan Collins' is one which *happens* to be false when uttered by me, but *could* have been true. How can this be?

Most of us have a fairly good grip on what it means to say that I could have been somewhere else, but only a hazy idea of what it means to say that I could have been a different person from who I am. Or do we? Most of us surely have had thoughts such as 'How would it have been if I had been born five years earlier?' or, more imaginatively, 'What would it have been like if I had been a woman and not a man?' Once again, the important thing is not how we would go about answering such questions, but the fact that they appear to make perfectly good sense. And if this is true, then I *can* give some meaning to the idea that I could have fitted other descriptions (descriptions which I don't in fact fit) *whilst being the same person that I am*. Of course, if I take very outlandish descriptions (could I have been a caveman, or a butterfly, or a prime number?) we run into difficulties about what 'I' is supposed to mean. As Ayer puts it, there are 'no fixed rules for determining what properties are essential to a person's being the person that he is'. But if we stick to the people around us – the people with respect to whom the problem of other minds arises in the first place – there is, Ayer argues, some sense in which I could have been, though I am not, any one of these other people. Furthermore, when it is stated that someone other than myself has an experience of a given sort, *it is no part of what is being asserted, that the experience belongs to someone else and not to me*; all that is being said is that it is the experience of someone *fitting a particular description*, a description which I logically *could* have fitted, but in fact do not. In this way, the argument from analogy can be defended against the original charge that other minds differ from e.g. other places, in that they can't be inspected. If we accept Ayer's reasoning, it seems that we are no more logically trapped in our own selves than we are trapped in our own period: we *could have* inspected another person's mind, if we had been that person (fitted the same descriptions), just as we *could have* inspected another place, had we been there.

Should this put our minds at rest and defeat the sceptic?

Three things suggest that it should not be seen as a final cure. The first concerns Ayer's insistence on the fitting of descriptions as being what constitutes personal identity; many philosophers (following Saul Kripke) would now disagree with the underlying assumptions made by Ayer, but this would get us into a rather technical area of philosophy, and we will not pursue it here.

The second is that, glancing back at the starting point of this enquiry, nothing which Ayer says has altered the fact that it is apparently logically possible that nobody except myself has any conscious experiences. What Ayer has done is to remove some of the obstacles to accepting observable facts about other people as evidence of their consciousness. But our original problem was that such evidence, however good of its kind, can never be shown to be *conclusive*, and that this has the effect of forcing us into the seemingly absurd position of having to take the solipsist seriously.

The third reservation which we may have about Ayer's formulation of the argument, is that it is little consolation to be told that statements about other minds are no worse off than statements about other times or other places, if, like the more radical type of solipsist, we are tempted to doubt these latter as well! For the solipsist can easily reply that, not only does he have no evidence that there are other minds apart from his own, but that he equally has no evidence that there are any states of affairs at all, which are not really just states of his own mind.

We may be beginning to suspect that the solipsist does indeed possess a trump card, and that no amount of argument can force him to budge from his original sceptical position. Indeed, there is something about scepticism of all kinds which at first presents this aspect. The sceptic apparently cannot be defeated so long as, in response to every reply we make to him, he simply says 'How do you know?' In the next chapter, however, we will look at a very different approach from that of the analogy argument, though it will be seen to have close connections with the views of Rorty, and the 'mentalistic stance' idea, explained earlier in this chapter.

4: Wittgenstein and the private language argument

The approach which will be outlined in this chapter is that suggested by some of the work of Ludwig Wittgenstein (1889-1951), an Austrian-born philosopher who spent most of his philosophical career in England. Wittgenstein has probably been the greatest single influence on British and American philosophy in the latter part of this century. His earlier philosophy is encapsulated in the *Tractatus Logico-Philosophicus* (1921), and the best-known work of his later period is the *Philosophical Investigations* (published posthumously in 1953). It is with the later work that we shall be concerned here, and especially with a few passages in the *Investigations* which have come to be known collectively as the Private Language Argument, for reasons which will become clear. These passages were probably not originally intended by Wittgenstein as a response to the problem of other minds, but the argument, if accepted, is very rich in its ramifications, and extends to this topic among others. There are also many different interpretations of the passages in question, though it is neither possible nor desirable to discuss them all here. What will be presented, then, is a fairly orthodox account of the argument, giving prominence to those aspects of it which are most relevant to our purposes. For this reason, the argument will be paraphrased rather than given in Wittgenstein's own words.

using language and making judgements
To begin, we recognize the way in which the making of *judge-*

ments depends on our being able to use *language*. Ours is, it seems, the only species capable of using language, in the full sense. By saying 'in the full sense' we mean that human beings can employ a connected system of conventional signs to communicate. It may be true that some other animals communicate by signs, such as screeching when some danger is present. Why should we not call this real language? The two words 'connected' and 'conventional' supply the answer. 'Conventional' means that the signs used have no natural connection with the thing being talked about. The word 'water', for example, is in no way *essentially* connected with the liquid stuff to which it refers. The French use the word *eau* and the Germans *Wasser*, and none of these words is any more correct or accurate than another: the word has no *intrinsic* meaning. This is unlike, for example, the way in which I might indicate the presence of water by making wavy motions with my hand, or show that I have a headache by grimacing and pointing to my head. It is also unlike the example of screeching to warn of danger: screeching is natural as opposed to conventional, not through being intrinsically connected with what it refers to, but because it is a spontaneous reaction rather than part of a learned and agreed code. By 'connected', we mean that language as used by human beings is a complex arrangement of signs which can be used in an unlimited variety of combinations with each other. We can distinguish, for example, between different *kinds* of danger: an earthquake, a large earthquake, a mad bull, a mad black bull, a black bull with large horns, a white bull with large horns, a black bull with small horns, and so on. This endless possibility of making distinctions and forming combinations of them using different parts of speech and grammatical constructions, is the other thing which seems to characterize genuine language and distinguish it from more primitive forms of communication. This difference between 'real' language and these primitive forms may, of course, be at bottom only one of degree, but it is none the less real for that.

What has this got to do with the possibility of making judgements? The important thing to recognise here is that a creature without language cannot, strictly speaking, be either right or wrong about something's being the case. This may sound odd at first, for cannot a cat, for example, spring at a leaf mistaking it for a mouse, and then walk away disappointed? Well, certainly a cat can make a mistake, but what is being claimed is that this is not a mistake *about something's being the case*. To make a mistake about what is the case, a mistake of fact, is to apply the wrong concept in a particular situation, and the cat cannot be said to possess the *concept* of a mouse in general, though it is usually able to recognise one in a given instance. We may say that the cat knows *how* to recognize a mouse, but not that it knows *that* such-and-such a thing is a mouse.

To make this clearer, let's take another example. I know *how* to ride a bicycle, though I do not know *that* certain things are the case concerning the way it is done. When the bicycle threatens to fall over in one direction, I turn the handlebars the opposite way, though I have never (until this moment) reflected that this is what I do. And when this happens, I am not making a judgement about what is the case: I just *do* it. If I fail to right the bicycle and it topples over, I have not made a mistake *of fact*, though I have of course made a mistake. Now I might, if I did enough research into it, be able to come up with a set of principles which would allow me to make judgements of fact concerning what is going on in such a situation. Then, if I were sufficiently quick thinking, I could say, 'Ah, the bicycle is leaning to the left at an angle of sixty degrees to the horizontal, on a fifteen degree adverse camber, with a radius of twenty yards, so it requires a five-eighths clockwise turn of the handlebars to right it'. And if I still toppled over I might say, 'Oh dear, it should have been *seven*-eighths!' In other words, I can now accuse myself of having made an error regarding a matter of fact, as opposed to just having done something foolish. The point is that my new-found ability to make a judgement of fact here depends on my having acquired the appropriate concepts, and this in turn depends on having mastered the use of certain linguistic terms such as 'degrees', 'clockwise', and 'adverse camber'.

If we are still not convinced that making judgements of fact is dependent on being a language user, consider finally the familiar word 'red'. Could I possess the concept of redness without knowing how to use the word 'red'? In one sense I obviously could, since a Frenchman certainly possesses the concept of redness, though he may never have heard the word 'red': this is because the word 'rouge' expresses the very same concept. But what about someone who had *no* word for what we understand by 'red'?

If we are tempted to think that he might nevertheless possess the concept of redness, secretly and incommunicably, let us ask how, even in his own terms, he could be right or wrong in employing the concept. In the case of our public concept which manifests itself in the use of the word 'red', we have a pretty good idea of what range of the colour spectrum constitutes the extension of the concept. At the borderlines we may disagree with each other, saying 'No, that's brown', or 'I'd call that orange'. Far from casting doubt on our grasp of the concept, this is actually one way in which the concept gains such sharpness as it has. For the boundaries, and the way in which it connects, in terms of differences and similarities, with surrounding concepts, are what give it its point. Hence our insistence on language being conventional, the result of an agreement to use signs in a particular way, and systematically connected, which is to say that words, and thereby concepts, gain their significance from the way they fit into a system of interrelated signs and concepts. A person who lacked the word 'red' could not possess the concept which we signify by it, for the reason that there could be no sense in describing her as either right or wrong about what colour an object, let's say an apple, is: all that her 'judgement' would boil down to, would be the idea that the apple 'is the colour that it is' (i.e. whatever colour she sees when she looks at it). And this is no judgement at all, since it is a mere truism, which *cannot* be false.

Of course, she might regard herself as making the 'judgement' that the apple is the same colour as the one she saw yesterday. But what can she suppose herself to mean by 'the same'? How alike in colour do two apples have to be in order to be 'the same colour' in her book? The answer surely is that since she has not learned when and when not to apply the word, the concept has no genuine extension for her – she cannot say where its application begins and ends, and therefore nothing will count as her being right or wrong in a given case, so nothing will count as her making a judgement about it. For the same reason, nothing will count as a right or wrong way of portraying something by gestures, or of emitting a spontaneous screech. We may regard as borderline the case of an intelligent animal which has been trained to respond in a given way to all and only those things which we call red. This brings us to the next stage in the argument.

the impossibility of a private language
Having seen how the making of judgements depends on our using language, we may now ask: what, apart from the right sort of brain structure etc., which we will look at in chapter 9, is necessary in order for one to be able to possess a language? And one answer which Wittgenstein gives is: the company of other language users. To see why this might be so, let us ask what it might mean to say that someone had a *private language*.

Many crude theories about how we acquire language suggest that it is, at bottom, a matter of mentally 'pinning labels' on things. The labels happen, of course, to be words in the language with which we have been brought up. But, according to this crude account, there is no logical reason why we should not do it in the absence of any other language users, merely by inventing our own labels. Now some versions of this rather naive theory involve thinking that the logically primary use of language is in labelling *one's own experiences* (private feelings, sensations, etc.), and that it is only secondarily that we can talk about external, public objects, by 'constructing' them out of the basic, uninterpreted experiences. On first sight, all this looks very straightforward and plausible: the development of understanding, according to this picture, is from simple to complex, from inner to outer, from oneself to other things. This is, however, roughly the reverse of the logical order of things as Wittgenstein teaches us to see them.

Notice, first of all, the difference between the weaker and the stronger forms of the naive view sketched above. The version which only says that language learning could be done in the absence of other language users, presupposes that you could, in such a case, invent a 'private language' known to you alone, with your own words for the objects around you. Having done this, you would then be in a position to teach that language to others. There are reasons for thinking that constructing such a private language would in fact be almost impossibly hard, unless you didn't already know *something* about language and languages. We need not go into these here. What is important is that, if you *did* succeed in inventing the language, it would be just a language like other languages, which could be learned and taught by other people. Consider, however, the stronger form which says that language is ultimately about our own sensations and suchlike. If I speak a language in which the words refer to private experiences of mine, it follows that this language is not teachable to anybody else, since the objects to which the basic terms of the language refer are not accessible to anyone other than myself. Ask, for example, how you could go about teaching another person the meaning of the word 'red', if 'red' functioned as a name for a certain quality of a patch in your own private visual field. There would be no way in which you could point out a red thing to that person, since private sensations are not the kind of thing at which you can point. In this way, a language which functioned like this would be *essentially private*: nobody else could *possibly* learn it. And if ordinary languages like English do function in this way, there must be a sense in which we each have our own language: a sense in which there must be as many 'English languages' as there are speakers of English. This is a tenable view, provided we can make sense of the idea of a private language in the first place. And this is precisely what Wittgenstein denied.

We will remember from the last section how the use of language is important for thought, because of the way in which it allows us to *fix the extension* of concepts: to agree on which cases are instances of them and which are not, and on what it is that makes the difference between something's being and not being an instance. This aspect of language Wittgenstein considers as an example of 'rule following'. Following a rule is the opposite of such things as acting in a purely instinctive way, as most animals do. Rule-governed activities are ones which involve acting according to some principle which tells us which things count as following the rule and which things count as going against it; which gives us an idea of what the difference consists in, between something's according with or not according with the rule. The rules of grammar are like this, and so perhaps are the rules of mathematics. So also are the rules which connect words in the language with things in the world – the semantic rules.

Now what would it be like to have only *private rules*? *Wittgenstein considers this hypothetical situation:*

> Let us imagine the following case. I want to keep a diary about the recurrence of a certain sensation. To this end I associate it with the sign 'S' and write this sign in a calender for every day on which I have the sensation. – I will remark first of all that a definition of the sign cannot be formulated. – But I can still give myself a kind of ostensive definition. – How? Can I point to the sensation? Not in the ordinry sense. But I speak, or write the sign down, and at the same time I concentrate my attention on the sensation – and so, as it were, point to it inwardly. – But what is this ceremony for? For that is all it seems to be! A definition surely serves to establish the meaning of a sign. Well, that is done precisely by the concentration of my attention; for in this way I impress on myself the connexion between the sign and the sensation. – But 'I impress it upon myself' can only mean: this process brings it about that I remember the connexion *right* in the future. But in the present case I have no criterion of correctness. One would like to say: whatever is going to seem right to me is right. And that only means that here we can't talk about 'right'.

This insistence on the fact that, in genuine rule following, there must be a distinction between what is right following of the rule, and what merely *seems* right, is typical of Wittgenstein during this period, and is crucial for the understanding of the Private Language Argument. If I find myself attempting to follow a rule which is mine alone, how do I tell whether I am following it correctly? On the one hand, I am the tutee who is learning how to recognize which cases do accord with the rule and which do not; on the other hand, I am also the authority of whether a given case is a genuine instance or not. This is paradoxical.

Wittgenstein's response to this is to claim that a private rule is no rule at all – that in order to engage in genuinely rule-governed activity, we need to be members of a *community* which upholds that rule and which is the authority on what makes the difference between following it and departing from it. Here, it is important to note that a 'rule', in this sense, does not mean something like a *law*, or *regulation* – it is not something which is enforced, which tells us *what to do*, but a principle which tells us *how to do* something. We will see more of this distinction in chapter 10. There are two aspects to the insistence on the need for a community of rule followers. One is the fact that, in a community, there exists the possibility of a *public check* on one's own understanding of the rule. The need for such a check arises out of the fact that unorthodox interpretations of any given rule are always possible. And this is to be understood in the strict logical sense: we can never be fully certain that another person understands a particular rule in the way that we do.

Suppose, for example, that we teach someone a rule by showing him a sequence which begins

2,4,6,8...

and then encourage him to continue the sequence in the same way. He will probably go on

10,12,14,16...

which suggests that he has understood the rule as corresponding to the instruction 'Add 2 at each step'. But he may, for instance, continue with

10,14,18,22...

If we point out to him that he is not continuing in the same way, he might reply that he took the rule to correspond to 'Add 2 up to 10, and after that add 4', and that he had been applying this rule all along. Thus, what counts as 'doing the same' is itself going to depend on what rule is being applied. So we cannot appeal to the notion of sameness to explain how we are following the same rule. Now since any such rule will have a potentially infinite number of instances, and we can only ever present someone with a finite selection of them, it follows that we can never be wholly certain that someone understands the rule in the same way that we do: there will always be an infinite number of cases in which his interpretation could diverge from ours.

At this point, some people will be tempted to say, 'But surely he can simply *tell* us what he understands the rule to be'. Can he not, for example, just say 'I'm adding two at each step', or 'I'm adding two until I get to ten, and after that four'? And since this is possible, why can't we merely do the obvious thing, which is to reach a verbal agreement on which rule we are using on any given occasion? The reason why this is no solution illustrates how deep the Wittgensteinian notion of rule following goes. For the verbal behaviour involved in telling someone which rule one is following, is also a rule-governed activity. And if we choose to be sceptical about whether two people are following the same mathematical rule, in order to be consistent we must be equally sceptical about whether they are using the same linguistic rules when they discuss which rule is being meant. How, then, can we ever be certain that any of us are following the same rule as one another? Or for that matter, how can a person ever be sure what rule *he himself* is following? For none of us can have considered every possible case of any such rule which he claims to follow. Of course, in practice we have no problem: on the whole, our interpretations tend to coincide with each other in those instances which we actually encounter. And where they do not, we can nearly always make the appropriate adjustments. Herein lies one possible solution to the problem of what has come to be known as 'rule scepticism'.

We may conclude that what it is for a number of people to be following the same rule is, not for each of them to have the same inner, private (and undiscovered even to the person in question) *interpretation*, but simply for them to *agree in practice*: this is the importance of the possibility of a 'public check'. Philosophers who call themselves Wittgensteinians tend to differ on the amount of weight which they place on the idea of a public check; and some are prepared to go further than others in regarding the community of agreement as all there is to having a genuine rule.

As indicated above, there is, however, another aspect to the need for other language users as a pre-condition for the acquisition of language. If we accept the impossibility of making a rule fully explicit, even to oneself, then there must come a point at which we can offer no further explanation of the rule in question, except by giving examples of what counts as following that rule in a certain (finite) number of cases. In a famous passage, Wittgenstein says:

> This was our paradox: no course of action could be determined by a rule, because every course of action be made out to accord with the rule. The answer was: if everything can be made to accord with the rule, then it can also be made out to conflict with it. And so there would be neither accord nor conflict here. It can be seen that there is a misunderstanding here from the mere fact that in the course of our argument we give one interpretation after another; as if each one contented us for at least a moment, until we thought of yet another standing behind it. What this shows is that there is a way of grasping a rule which is *not* an *interpretation*, but which is exhibited in what we call 'obeying a rule' and 'going against it' in actual cases.

The emphasis on the rule as manifested in actual cases is very much what we saw above. When Wittgenstein says that there must be a way of grasping a rule which is not an interpretation, a further point is being made. We cannot know what counts as following a rule in *all* its instances, since we cannot possibly consider all of them. Yet we are tempted to think that in some way when we grasp a rule, all the instances of it are in a sense already fixed. Wittgenstein explains this in the following way:

> 'All the steps are already taken' means: I no longer have any choice. The rule, once stamped with a particular meaning, traces the lines along which it is to be followed through the whole of space. – But if something of this sort really were the case, how would it help? No; my description only made sense if it were to be understood symbolically. – I should have said: *This is how it strikes me*. When I obey a rule, I do not choose. I obey the rule *blindly*.

A way of grasping a rule which is 'not an interpretation' is, then, a matter of following 'blindly'. When we come to the point at which we can give no further explanation of the rule, all that is left is to appeal to what comes naturally. And the reason why we can do this, is because of the habits which have been instilled into us by our *training* in rule following. This appeal to training brings out an aspect of what is necessary for genuine rule following, which goes even beyond the idea that we require our applications of a rule to be checked by a community of rule followers. What it suggests is that we have no real claim to grasp rules at all, unless there is some way in which we initially internalized them: some way, that is, in which we could be said to have learned, to have acquired, the rule in question. And making it up oneself is not, in this sense, an authentic way of acquiring a rule: for in such a case one would have to invent not just a rule itself, as though it could be captured in its entirety by a single mental act, but what is to count as an instance of it in *every* given case.

Training in rule following is not possible, if we accept the above, for an isolated individual. If what has been said is true, the use of language, properly speaking, is a collective and social phenomenon. What repercussions does this have for the original question which motivated this discussion of Wittgenstein?

the case against solipsism

We are now in a position to see why it has been claimed by some that the Private Language Argument, if we accept it, shows that solipsism cannot be correct. For if the making of judgements depends on being able to use language, and if language, as a rule-governed activity, requires a public check and training in the following of a rule, then the absence of other people means that, despite appearances, one could not be genuinely making judgements if one were the only intelligence in the world. Try to imagine such a world: a world of which oneself is the only genuine occupant. Of course, all the other people will be there also, at least in appearance; but they will be merely empty shells with an 'outside' but no 'inside'. Only oneself has an 'inside'. In such a position, how would one ever know the meaning of a word or symbol?

This is a serious question. There would be no difference between following a rule and merely *thinking* one was following a rule; no difference, as Wittgenstein puts it, between something's *being* right and *seeming* right. The idea of there being any 'right' collapses, through its being indistinguishable from whatever would seem right to oneself at a given time. Judgements will, then, be impossible; for there being no difference between applying a concept rightly and applying it wrongly, in other words no difference between making a correct and an incorrect judgement, destroys what is central to the whole idea of a judgement.

The upshot of all this, is that *if* it is true that you are really thinking, making genuine judgements, having coherent thoughts, *then* solipsism is false. But why need one accept the first statement – that one really is genuinely thinking? Could one not be sceptical and agnostic about both of them? The answer is that one could not. For even to suspect or consider the notion that solipsism *might* be true is to make a coherent judgement. On this account, even to take solipsism seriously is to be in a muddle about what one can and can't, logically speaking, take seriously. It is very like the idea of judging oneself to be mad – not as a real madman might in a rare moment of lucidity, but judging oneself to be totally insane whilst one is making the judgement itself. It is an impossible judgement to make, precisely because if it were true, it would follow that it was not a genuine judgement (provided we understand 'totally insane' to entail 'not able to make judgements').

This, then, is the case which a certain brand of Wittgensteinian philosopher might offer to us about solipsism. What are we to say of it? First of all, how sure are we that the notion of a public check on our use of concepts, and our training in the use of them, do really require there to be other conscious people. Will not the empty shells of the solipsist's world do just as well? After all, if I cannot distinguish a world in which the other people are real and have 'insides', from one in which they are mere automata and only have 'outsides', what difference could it possibly make to anything? The answer to this, is that the question of whether any genuine rule following is going on is not an empirical one, that is, not one which can be settled by an further *experiences,* but a logical one. And, if the Private Language Argument is correct, then rule following in one person entails that there is some rule following going on elsewhere. Unfortunately, this has a slightly embarrassing consequence for the Wittgensteinian, since it commits us to the view that *at least one other person* is conscious, and therefore to maintaining simply that the total number of conscious beings in the world is at least *two*! Fortunately, however, the existence of one other conscious being bodes quite well for the rest of them, for the very reason that two is somehow an inherently unlikely number. In any case, it tells us that solipsism is not open to us, and this is what we first started out to settle. Later, in chapter 10, an argument will be made out for the view that rule following demands consciousness, which was the weak link here.

In the meantime, should we be convinced by the Private Language Argument itself? One can imagine an objection to it which goes something like this. A single individual trying to follow a rule all by herself will never be in a position to know whether she is following the rule correctly or not, for there will never be any public verification. But how is an entire community in a better position? For since we are considering logical possibilities (things which are possible since they are not self-contradictory, but which may be extremely improbable), could not a whole community be misled about the rule, and in the exact same way, so that the divergence could not be detected? And if so, doesn't this show that one man would, from a logical point of view, have been as good as a million in the first place?

This is a tempting objection, but it arises out of having missed the point of the Private Language Argument. For the argument is *not* to the effect that one person could be mistaken about how he applies the rule, whilst a number of people are more likely to be correct. Its point is that *the whole idea of correctness* becomes meaningless when applied to the case of a lone individual. The difference between there being one consciousness and more than one is not just that two heads are better than one; it is the difference between being able to make a distinction between what *is* right and what *seems* right, and not being able to make it.

Before leaving the topic of the Private Language Argument, let us go back to what was said above about the fact that the argument demands the premise that we really are, in fact, capable of making judgements. In other words, the argument is *conditional* in form: it says '*If* there are any real judgements being made, *then* solipsism is false. We noticed that it is impossible to deny the first statement, since to do so would itself be to make a judgement. But there is something fishy about this. It is true that *I* cannot doubt that *I* am making judgements. But I *can* doubt whether someone else is doing so, and he can doubt that I am. The reason for this is simply that there is no logical guarantee that *any given* person is really thinking, even oneself. The proposition 'It is impossible for me to doubt that I am making judgements' does not add up to the conclusion 'Therefore I must be making judgements'. One knows perfectly well what it is for someone such as a lunatic not really to be making judgements. And one therefore knows *what it would be* for this to be the case with oneself – maybe at some future time, for example. Thus, one knows what would be being asked by the question 'Am I really making judgements?', and therefore one knows in a sense what is meant by supposing that one might not be. Thus the argument still remains conditional in form: the conclusion that solipsism cannot be true continues to rest on the unverified premise that one is genuinely using concepts and making judgements. As premises go, however, this might be thought to be quite a strong one. At any rate, we know, if we accept Wittgenstein's argument, that there is no point in questioning it: we are stuck with it for all practical purposes, and therefore with that which follows from it.

An argument which has this kind of structure is often known as a *transcendental argument*. A transcendental argument says, in essence: 'We must suppose A to be the case; and if A is the case then B must be also, in order to make A possible'. Attention was drawn to transcendental arguments in the eighteenth century by the philosopher Immanuel Kant. We will be seeing more of Kant in chapter 8.

5: communication and interaction

The problem with which we began was: could a machine ever be capable of genuine conscious thought, and if so, how could we tell? We then recognized that there was a problem not just about how we can tell in the case of machines, but about how we know other *people* are conscious: and not just some borderline cases, like the badly brain damaged or comatose, but *all* other people. Now if Wittgensteinian philosophers are correct, who make out a case of the sort discussed in the last chapter, then we seem to have a transcendental argument to the effect that solipsism is false, and one has no choice but to accept that other people have conscious thoughts in just the way one does oneself. No one has a privileged status in this respect, just by virtue of being 'number one' as far as *he* is concerned. But where does this get us as regards our original question? How can the Wittgensteinian position help us in deciding what kind of thing might lead us to suspect that a *machine* might be having thoughts in just the way we do?

animation and the Turing test
It was pointed out in chapter 2, that the kind of machines to which people are often tempted to attribute consciousness are ones which just sit somewhere handling data, and which are not animate in any real sense. It was also noticed, that it is animation which gives us the clue to when a human being is conscious and when not. However, in chapter 2 we concluded that it would be an easy matter to build a machine which

jumped around and suchlike, but to which no one would have the least temptation to attribute consciousness. It must now be recognized that this was much too short a way with the point about animation. For there is more to genuine animation than simply doing what a jack-in-a-box or 'nodding dog' does. And what is required over and above mere movement and simple responses, we have seen in discussing Wittgenstein. It is the ability to *communicate*: to enter into a dialogue, or into a shared practice with other creatures.

One thing, then, which might quite rightly lead us to suspect that there was some real thinking going on in a machine, would be if we found ourselves reacting to the machine as though it were a conscious being, due to the likeness of *its* responses to those of a human person. If, that is, we found ourselves entering into what seemed like real communication with it. In particular, if we found it impossible to distinguish between communicating with the machine and communication with a human being, this tendency would be at its strongest. This was, in fact, the test suggested by the pioneer of computing, Alan Turing, in 1950. Recognizing that questions about whether machines can think are apt to raise the spectre of solipsism, and recognizing also that even those who completely reject the idea that machines can think nonetheless wish to avoid the solipsist position, Turing concluded that there must be some *test* for whether a thing is really thinking or not – a test which most humans beings pass, and which most, if not all, machines don't.

The test which Turing came up with was precisely that of finding out whether communication with the machine was indistinguishable from communication with a human being – whether a person could be 'fooled' by a machine. Of course, if you really wanted to carry out the test, you would need to have both a computer and a human being able to communicate with a second human being in the same way, for example via a series of questions and answers on a terminal, with the second human being having to guess which was which. But the point of the test is primarily theoretical: it is meant to establish the *principle* that the criterion of when something is really thinking, is whether or not that thing can communicate, answer questions and so on, in a way which is indistinguishable from that of a human person.

One passage from Turing's writing is well known in this respect. He is replying to the arguments of Sir Geoffrey Jefferson, a critic of artificial intelligence, who said in 1949:

> Not until a machine can write a sonnet or compose a concerto because of thoughts and emotions felt, and not by the chance fall of symbols, could we agree that machine equals brain – that is, not only write it but know it had written it. No mechanism could feel (and not merely artificially signal, an easy contrivance) pleasure at its successes, grief...bewarmed by flattery, be made miserable by its mistakes, be charmed by sex, be angry or depressed when it cannot get what it wants.

Turing first asks how Jefferson himself would tell whether another human being really had certain abilities, or only the semblance of them. He says:

> I am sure that Professor Jefferson does not want to adopt the extreme and solipsist point of view. Probably he would be quite willing to adopt the imitation game as a test. The game...is frequently used in practice under the name of *viva voce* to discover whether someone really understands something or has 'learnt it parrot fashion'.

Turing goes on to give an example of an exchange between an 'interrogator' and a 'witness', in which the interrogator is attempting to establish whether some lines written by the witness were written with genuine understanding or not. The gist of the argument is that if, in a situation like this, the interrogator cannot distinguish between a machine as 'witness' and a human being, then there are no grounds for holding the machine's intelligence to be less a case of genuine thought than that of a human person. He concludes:

> In short, then, I think that most of those who support the argument from consciousness could be persuaded to abandon it rather than be forced into the solipsist position. They will then probably be willing to accept our test. I do not wish to give the impression that I think there is no mystery about consciousness...But I do not think these mysteries necessarily need to be solved before we can answer the question with which we are concerned in this paper.

The question with which Turing actually began the paper was simply 'Can machines think?' However, he considered this question so obscure that he proposed to 'replace' it with the question of whether a machine could fool people consistently in the above way. From the final remarks in the passage, it is clear that Turing is not one of those who reject the concept of consciousness entirely. He does, however, want to divorce it from the notion of thinking. We shall be looking, in chapters 10 and 11, at some reasons for thinking that this cannot be done. We may consider here, however, that Turing's reason for wishing to make this move is one which we have already rejected. It is that in Turing's view the insistence on consciousness as the important element goes hand-in-hand with the view that the only way of telling whether a creature thinks is to *be* that creature. For Turing, the person who interprets the above question as asking 'Are machines *conscious*?' is forced into a solipsistic position. Here Turing's reasoning is weak. For there can be evidence of consciousness – the symptoms we talked of above – which do not rely at all on *being* the thing or person in question. Some of them are, in fact, precisely those captured by the Turing Test itself.

It is quite reasonable, therefore, for those who want to insist on consciousness as the crucial element in 'real' thought, to adopt the Turing Test as suggested: but not as a replacement for the harder question about consciousness. Rather, as an indication of the answer to that question in a given case. We may, of course, want to insist on other ingredients besides those pointed to by Turing. For example, there is the question of animation, which was discussed in chapter 2, and earlier in this chapter. We shall see later that sentience must also be considered important in any candidate for consciousness. Symptoms, then, there are a-plenty. And Wittgenstein has shown us a way of connecting the symptoms with the condition of which they are symptoms. For what the Wittgensteinian argument demonstrates, if it is correct, is that the fact that no amount of these symptoms *logically add up to* the conclusion that a given creature is conscious does *not* mean that we are seriously threatened with solipsism. It is time now to look further at some of the symptoms themselves, and at some of the human inventions which may be thought to exhibit them.

programs that talk to us

Inevitably, attempts have been made to create computer programs which are capable of passing a test such as the Turing Test: programs which will cause a machine to converse with someone in a believably human way. Many of the early language-using programs involved no more than a question-and-answer type situation. They merely answered a very large number of questions on a given topic, such as football, or geography, or whatever. Naturally, no one could be fooled into thinking that such a thing was human – change the subject and they are lost completely! Others, however, were broader and more advanced.

One of these became well known as a just credible human substitute. It has actually been known to fool an employee of the company where it was developed. This program is called ELIZA, after Eliza Doolittle, the heroine of Shaw's *Pygmalion*, who was taught to speak 'good' English. The reason why ELIZA is able to create, up to a point, the illusion of genuine interaction, is that in place of having a data base of facts on a given topic, or even on general knowledge, it takes its material from the conversation of the other person, the user. A program which merely used its own information would soon be 'found out' when the interlocutor suddenly changed the subject, or alluded to one of those trivial but universally shared items in our culture which are hard to pin down in a data base. The beauty of ELIZA is that *it* asks the questions, and talks about whatever the user wants to talk about.

An example of the beginning of a real conversation with ELIZA is the following (ELIZA's responses are in capital letters):

> HELLO. PLEASE TELL ME ABOUT YOUR PROBLEM.
> I keep getting headaches.
> YOU SAY YOU KEEP GETTING HEADACHES.
> I think it's because of my job.
> YOUR JOB?

Yes.
PLEASE TELL ME MORE.
I get a lot of trouble from customers.
CAN'T YOU ELABORATE ON THAT?
They make a lot of demands on me.
I AM NOT SURE I UNDERSTAND YOU FULLY.
They cause lots of stress.
PLEASE GO ON.
I think I need a holiday.
WHAT WOULD IT MEAN TO YOU IF YOU GOT A HOLIDAY?
It would give me a rest.
WHAT DOES THAT SUGGEST TO YOU?
I work too hard.
......etc.

It will be noticed that ELIZA's conversation resembles that of a psychiatrist talking to a patient. It is significant that this was the intention with which the program was written, since the

psychiatrist-patient situation is one in which it is normal for one party, the psychiatrist, to make conversation which centres entirely on the other party's topics. Such an interview also tends to keep off 'hard facts' and revolve more around feelings and reactions, so that a detailed knowledge of actual things (as opposed to what the patient feels or thinks about them) is unnecessary.

But when we turn to general conversation, of the kind which usually leads us to believe that we have encountered a conscious human being, the results are much worse, often to the point of being comical. Consider another actual conversation with ELIZA, in which the user did not play the part of a disturbed person anxious to talk about his own feelings, but that of a normal person looking for a conversation:

> HELLO. PLEASE TELL ME YOUR PROBLEM.
> I can't find a bottle opener.
> HOW DO YOU KNOW YOU CAN'T FIND A BOTTLE OPENER?
> I've looked for half an hour.
> I AM NOT SURE I UNDERSTAND YOU FULLY.
> I have looked for the bloody bottle opener for the past half hour.
> YOU SAY YOU HAVE LOOKED FOR THE BLOODY BOTTLE OPENER FOR THE PAST HALF HOUR.
> Yes.
> PLEASE GO ON.
> ....etc.

As Professor Margaret Boden has put it:

> such 'speaking machines' do not behave like someone conversing in her native language. Rather, they resemble a person resorting to trickery and semantic sleight-of-hand in order to hide her own lack of understanding of a foreign tongue.

There is, of course, no reason *in principle* why a combination of this sort of interrogation of the user, with a phenomenally large data base of everyday facts, should not produce something realistic. But 'in principle' is a very big qualification to make.

nuts and bolts
Although it might be possible, in principle, to write a program

which will really allow a machine to simulate the linguistic and other behaviour of a human being, there is another factor which might make us want to hesitate before accepting that such a machine would really be thinking. This is the curious fact that the temptation to regard a machine as really thinking tends to go away once we know in detail how it works – once we get down to the 'nuts and bolts'. One reason, in fact, why so many people really do suspect that computers might be consciously thinking, is that their circuitry is electronic, hidden, and not understood by most people. If it worked by clockwork, or wind power, or water power, probably no one would be interested in making this claim at all. But to someone who actually does know how a computer is put together, how a 'talking program' is written, there arises, at least as yet, no question of attributing conscious thought to it. Nor is it likely to in the foreseeable future. Of course, to some journalists, we are always on the brink of some breakthrough which is going to be the 'great leap forward'; computer scientists and artificial intelligence workers are, on the whole, more cautious in their optimism.

Herein lies a curious anomaly. For we appear not even to apply the same standards of evidence to human beings as we do to artifacts. Whereas knowing in detail how a machine works is likely to make us less inclined to suspect it of anything like conscious thought, the same is not true as regards people. The discoveries of medical science concerning the functioning of the human body do not have the effect of making us more sceptical about other minds. Here, of course, the Argument from Analogy does have some purchase, which explains the anomaly: for the knowledge that at least one physical mechanism put together in our shape is capable of consciousness does remove any feeling of inherent unlikelihood with regard to the possibility of such mechanisms supporting conscious thought in general. But if the analogy argument can get us this far, it still does not follow immediately that we are entitled to attribute consciousness to other physical mechanisms just insofar as they resemble our-selves. For this, we require some further argument.

It ought now to be obvious that one aspect of this will lie in the question of what it is for a creature to be actually understanding what it is doing, and in particular understanding the language it uses. The kinds of systems we glanced at above are not such that one would suspect them of genuinely attaching meaning to the utterances they produce, however sophisticated these utterances might look on the surface. To put this another way, systems of this type have no real *semantics*: the meanings of their utterances are only meanings imposed by us, the creators and users of them, and not meanings to the machine or system itself. And one reason why the vast majority of artifacts cannot seriously be suspected of possessing any semantics, is that they do not interact in the relevant ways with the 'outside' world. They cannot pin meanings on words in the way that we can, because they do not have genuine access to the things which the words *stand for* in the way that we do. We shall see more of this later, especially in chapter 10.

For the moment, however, we will need to embark on another extended detour. For before beginning to draw sweeping conclusions about what conditions are necessary and/or sufficient for conscious thought, we really ought to ask what, in general, is supposed to be the relation between a physical organism such as a human being, and the conscious thought of which it is capable. And this, as many readers will probably have already realised, is none other than the traditional 'Mind-Body Problem': the question of the relation between the mental and physical aspects of a person. In the next three chapters, therefore, we will be looking at some common approaches to this philosophical problem. If, at some points, it begins to look as though this detour is in danger of rendering the issue less rather than more clear, it is important (as always) to bear with the argument until it is possible to see in what direction it leads.

6: mind and matter

If the criteria for consciousness are something to do with the behaviour which a thing exhibits to other creatures, and its interactions with them, what significance we actually give to these things will depend to a large extent on the view which we take of the precise nature of the relation between mind and body, or between mind and outward behaviour. In other words, it is all very well to say that there are 'criteria' for recognizing the presence of consciousness; but what we understand by this rather loose term will be determined by our general view of (to put it first of all in a deliberately traditional way) the connection between mind and matter. This is, of course, an enormously old philosophical problem, or cluster of problems, which originally arose only with regard to human beings and the way in which their mental features relate to their bodies, physical make-up and bodily behaviour. Only by seeing how the matter stands when dealing with human beings, then, will we be likely to throw light on how it stands when we come to deal with machines.

In order to understand what choice of views is available here, and how the different views would fit into the question about minds and machines, let us look (though we will only be scratching the surface) at the chief theories which have been propounded. We will divide them into two groups, the first corresponding to what are known as *dualist* theories, and the second to what are called *monist* theories. Roughly speaking, dualist theories see mind and matter as two fundamentally separate things, whereas monist theories hold that there is really only *one* thing – either mind, or matter, or something of which both mind and matter are aspects. We begin with the dualist theories, leaving monist accounts for the following two chapters.

Cartesian dualism

The most obvious, and in some ways the simplest, dualist theory is that of the French philosopher René Descartes (1596 –1650). When the word 'dualism' is mentioned to a philosophically trained person, the name of Descartes is the one which probably springs first to mind.

At the heart of Descartes' theory is the idea that the body and the mind are two quite different, though in some way connected, things. They are, to put it in the language of his time, different 'substances'. Descartes' central argument for this is as simple as it is initially appealing. Close your eyes, shut off your ears and other sense organs, and try to imagine yourself without a body. Suppose for a moment that nothing physical, nothing material, exists, and concentrate purely on your own consciousness. If you can do this, then Descartes thinks it follows that it is logically possible (i.e. involves no contradiction) that *you* should exist, even in the absence of your body, or indeed of any other physical thing. What remains is the immaterial, incorporeal *mind*.

In fact, we did not even need to close our eyes. For, as Descartes' initial position of scepticism (suspension of belief) emphasises, the *apparently* physical things around me which I see, hear, and so on, could themselves possibly be only ideas or illusions in my mind! And if this is how things stand, then we cannot escape the conclusion that the mind is a totally different and independent thing from the body. If the 'man in the street' knows anything at all about Descartes, he probably knows the famous phrase 'I think, therefore I am'. This is Descartes' way of saying that the one thing which I cannot doubt is my own existence, for the very act of doubting itself inevitably involves the existence of the person doing the doubting. Thus, I am first of all aware that I am conscious, that I have a *mind*, and only subsequently am I aware, by using my mind, that I have a body – that is, that there are physical items in the world which are uniquely and directly under my control, and are of special concern to me.

As we recognized earlier, Descartes does, of course, accept the existence of a connection between the mind and the body: naturally the mind must be able to control the bodily movements which are subject to our will, and the body must in turn be able to affect the mind, since much of what we know in our minds has to originate with the sense organs of the body. Rather quaintly to us, Descartes locates the chief intersection between the mind and the body in the pineal gland, a small organ in the brain. Whilst nobody now would take seriously this glandular explanation, there are many who are tempted – and it is not hard to see why, on first sight – by a Cartesian or neo-Cartesian form of dualism. Most philosophers these days, however, reject Descartes' account. Why?

Firstly, Descartes' case, at least as stated above, rests on a premise which is not fully articulated in his writing. This may be expressed as the assumption that wherever one thing, call it A, can be imagined without simultaneously imagining another thing B, then A and B must be different entities, with A not being dependent on B for its existence. Do we have to accept this? Take a simpler, though perhaps rather imperfect, example. Can you imagine fire without the presence of oxygen? In some sense, most of us probably can. Primitive man, when he imagined fire, would certainly not have imagined it as entailing the presence of oxygen, though obviously he could not have thought of it as oxygen-less either. Does it follow from this that fire and oxygen are two separate things, and that fire is in no way dependent for its existence on oxygen? Surely not, for we now know that fire in fact *is* burning oxygen. We cannot pretend that this brief argument constitutes any sort of final refutation of Descartes – his defenders would have much to say in reply. In order to follow this up, however, one would have to go to a specialist book or journal on the subject. All that has been done here is to sketch one possible approach to a rejection of Descartes' reasoning.

Malebranche and occasionalism

Now if we want to retain the idea that mind and matter are two separate things, and yet cannot bring ourselves to believe in some Cartesian-type mechanism whereby they interact, an obvious move would be to deny that they interact at all. This is the view taken by Nicolas Malebranche (1638-1715), who was himself greatly influenced by Descartes. The problem for the defender of such a view is, of course, to explain the *apparent* interaction of mind and body: in particular, the correspondence between our mental desires and volitions, and the physical effects which they seem to produce in our bodies. For example, I decide to pick up an apple which I see in front of me, because I want to eat it. This mental occurrence results in the movement of my arm as I reach out for it. Is there not surely something like a causal connection between the mental act of decision and the physical movement of the arm?

Malebranche says there is not; indeed he denies the existence of *any* causation in the sense in which most of us understand it. The apparent connection, according to him, is to be explained by the fact that God, noting my decision, brings it about that my arm moves. God, on Malebranche's view, directly brings about all those things which we normally think of as being caused by other things or events in the world. What we naturally regard as being the cause of an event is not, he maintains, the *true* cause at all, but only what he refers to as the *occasional* cause (the occasion of God's acting), hence the name given to his theory – occasionalism.

Malebranche has a clever, if not entirely convincing, argument for his thesis that we do not really cause our own bodily movements. He points out that if we did cause them ourselves, we would have to know *how* to do so. And from this it follows, on his account, that we would have to know about the workings of the human brain, the nerves, the muscles, and all that goes into producing the action. Clearly we do not know all this, and yet are somehow capable of performing considerable feats of dexterity. Therefore, he concludes, we cannot be directly responsible for these actions ourselves – they are brought about not by us, but by God acting 'on our behalf'. Conversely, the apparent causal effects which physical objects exert on our minds can be explained along the same lines. The regularity of the apparent 'laws' linking mental and physical occurrences can be accounted for by the fact that God has indeed laid down laws, though these only have the status of resolutions on His part to act in certain regular and predictable ways.

One obvious drawback which people find with occasionalism is that it requires us to bring in God to explain some quite familiar facts about the world, and that the explanation itself is highly counterintuitive. Malebranche, of course, would point out that reason requires us to believe that things happen in the way he describes, since any other way is logically ruled out by his argument. Yet the argument, as presented here, is not at all as watertight as he considered it to be. The best point at which to attack it would probably be the step from knowing how to perform an action to knowing some facts about human physiology. Philosophers today would, on the whole, be inclined to see a sharper distinction between knowing *how* (to do something) and knowing *that* (something is the case), and to hesitate before concluding that the former always implies the latter. Remember, in this connection, the bicycle example in chapter 4. However this may be, we will move on now to consider a rival theory of the relation between mind and body, propounded by a critic of Malebranche.

Leibniz and the pre-established harmony
This critic is Gottfried Leibniz (1646-1716). Leibniz both admired, and found fault with, the systems of Descartes and of Malebranche. He considered that Descartes had simply 'abandoned the struggle' when it came to explaining how mind and body can ever interact. And his view of Malebranche was that the latter had shown what could *not* be the case, without having explained what in fact *is*. That is, he accepted Malebranche's thesis that our bodily movements are not truly caused by our own mental acts of will, but found himself unable to agree with Malebranche's occasionalist explanation, according to which God must somehow step in at every point to salvage the appearance of genuine connection between things.

There is neither space nor necessity here to go into the whole of Leibniz's philosophy, even as regards the mind, but the outline of his theory concerning the relation between mind and body goes like this. The mental occurrences which make up the experience of the mind, arise entirely from its own nature and constitution. Similarly, the physical happenings which form the life of the body, are part of *its* nature, and come about only by physical laws. The apparent causal interaction between mind and body is brought about not, as Malebranche had argued, by the direct intervention of God on each occasion of ostensible interaction, but by a 'pre-established harmony' between the two processes. Whereas Malebranche regarded the 'laws' governing the coincidence of mental and physical events as merely resolutions on God's part to act on each individual occasion in a given way, Leibniz saw them as principles which God had set in motion and, having done so, could leave alone to fulfil their intended purposes, much as a watchmaker winds up a watch and leaves it to run, without constantly having to set it at the correct time.

Leibniz himself uses the analogy of two clocks to explain his view. If, he points out, two clocks are both so accurately made and so perfectly adjusted that they neither gain or lose at all, then both of them will always be doing corresponding things at the same time. One will be chiming eight just when the cuckoo is coming out of the other one eight times. This, Leibniz believes, is the real position regarding mind and body. Both are originally set in motion in such a way that they keep in perfect accord with each other. Thus, just at the time when I am resolving to eat an apple, my arm reaches out and picks one up – not because I actually cause it to do so, but because things are so divinely ordered that the two events coincide perfectly in time, with the result that we are tempted to attribute some further connection to them.

What can we say about Leibniz's theory? First of all, like Malebranche's it requires us not only to believe in God, but to believe that many ordinary facts about the world can only be explained by granting to God a special role in our scientific methodology. Leibniz argues, in effect, that his view is a neater, more elegant one than that of Malebranche. He says that the system he describes is 'more worthy' of God, and in this he is right. What we may doubt, however, is whether the thinkers of the period we have so far been considering were correct in seeing such a radical difficulty in explaining how unlike 'substances' can interact. And, even more fundamentally, whether they were right to think of mind and matter as two equally real and independent substances (types of thing) at all. These questions are of too great a scope for the present work, though some light might be shed on them by comparing the theories we have seen so far with some more recent ones which do not embody the same kinds of assumptions. The final theory which we shall consider in this chapter brings us much nearer to the present day, and certainly has a less theological flavour about it.

Huxley's epiphenomenalism

Although it sounds rather daunting, 'epiphenomenalism' just means the theory that mental events, although real, do not function as *causes*. We began by seeing how Descartes considered that mind and matter could *interact*, i.e. act *on each other*. Now whilst Malebranche and Leibniz both denied that any genuine interaction was going on, the nineteenth century English writer T.H. Huxley took the course of accepting the existence of causal interaction *in one direction only*. Although he regarded both matter and mind as real, in a sense matter was for him the 'more real', for he saw it as causing mental events, whereas mental events did not, he argued, cause physical ones.

Mental phenomena, then, according to Huxley, are 'epiphenomena', mere concomitants of physical action, with no causal power of their own. When it seems to us that a mental event, such as a conscious intention to put my hat on, is the cause of a physical event, namely the putting on of my hat, what actually happens is that the physical event is brought about, not by the conscious intention, but by the *physical counterpart*, in the brain or wherever, of the conscious intention. Thus, according to the epiphenomenalist, the man in the street tends to regard a mental event as being the cause of a physical event, whereas in fact a quite different physical event is the cause of them both. When this understandable confusion is remedied, we see that mind, or consciousness, is no more than a kind of ineffective froth given off by the more fundamental physical processes. In Huxley's words:

> It seems to me that in man, as in the brutes, there is no proof that any state of consciousness is the cause of change in the motion of the matter of the organism...it follows that our mental conditions are simply the symbols in consciousness of the changes which take place automatically in the organism; and that, to take an extreme illustration, the feeling which we call volition is not the cause of a voluntary act, but the symbol of that state of the brain which is the immediate cause of the act. We are conscious automata, endowed with free will in the only intelligible sense of that much-abused term – inasmuch as in many respects we are able to do as we like – but none the less parts of the great series of causes and effects...

It is worth spending a little time on a discussion of epiphenomenalism, since it is at first sight a very plausible theory, and is likely to have a good deal more initial appeal than the accounts discussed in this chapter so far. One aspect of it which attracts many people is its seemingly 'scientific' character, being able to do justice to the existence of conscious experience, whilst avoiding any ghostly or spiritual substance or mechanism.

What kind of objection, then, may be argued against epiphenomenalism? One is quite obvious, when it is pointed out: it certainly seems, in our, experience, that things turn out differently when we put conscious thought into them, from how they turn out without it. If I walk around the house without having my mind on it, or in my sleep, I tend to fall over, bump into things, and so on. Surely, the epiphenomenalist will say, but for all you know, it could just as easily be that you actually do things more efficiently when you have *that physical feature which gives rise to* the conscious feeling of wakefulness, attentiveness, etc.

This is, of course, a move which the epiphenomenalist can make with regard to any mental state which threatens to be causally efficacious. There are reasons, however, for hesitating before accepting it. Firstly, it must be remembered that if we accept this account of how things are, we pay as heavy a price for it as we do if we accept occasionalism or the pre-established harmony, in terms of the number of everyday beliefs we have to give up. Not only will my intention to put on my hat not be what brings it about that I put it on, but nobody will truly be said to have a drink because they feel thirsty, go to college because they want to learn French, or get married because they are in love: inverted commas will have to go round nearly everything.

Secondly, psycho-physical events present themselves to us in such a way that, not only is it the case that a conscious intention is invariably found to be followed (all other things being equal) by the physical action of which it was the intention; but further, that there is an intimate relationship between the two – what philosophers call an internal relation – one which is not just accidental but which somehow follows from the nature of the related things themselves. This is borne out by a matter of logic: the action, say, of 'waving to the woman next door' would not count as being this particular action, without the context provided by my intention. It might count as some other physically identical action, such as trying to swat a fly or fanning myself to keep cool, or it might not count as an action at all, if, for example, it was the result of a nervous tic. The nature of the resulting action, and therefore its (according to Huxley, physical) explanation will depend on the intention – *and on the intention itself, not its alleged physical counterpart*, since it simply makes no sense to suppose that the appropriate context could be provided by physical counterparts.

Of course, this does not prove that there are causes which are non-physical; but it does show at the very least that there are explanations which are not causal. These non-causal explanations may, like the one in the example above, be of a *contextual* kind, and it is this sort of explanation which cannot be handled by the epiphenomenalist, since he can neither accept it as it stands, since it is not a physical explanation, nor give an equivalent description of it in purely physical terms. It is not so much that we need mental events as causes, distinct from the physical events which they cause; it is rather that the character of the event cannot be properly understood without some reference to the fact that it has a mental, as well as a physical, side to it (i.e. some reference, not to the intention as the cause of the action in the sense that a stone may cause a broken window, but to the intention *with which the action was performed*, as making it the action which it is).

This should perhaps suggest to us that in dealing with an apparent case of mental cause giving rise to physical effect, we might be misleading ourselves by talking about *two* things and debating whether and how they interact. An internal relation such as that between intention and action is too close to admit of 'interaction' (the premises and conclusion of an argument don't *interact*, neither do the size and shape of a box). Should we perhaps not be looking in the direction of regarding an event such as an intentionally-performed action as a single thing rather than two things welded insecurely together? It is to this line of enquiry that we turn in the next chapter.

7: just one thing: monism

As we saw in the last chapter, the alternative to a dualist account of the relation between mind and body is a *monist* account. A monist holds the opinion that there are not *really* two things – mind and body – but only one thing which somehow presents itself as a duality, or encourages us to see a duality where there is none. Monist views may be divided into categories, according to what they consider the one thing in question to be. We may start by separating them into just three categories, depending on whether they regard the one 'real' substance as (a) mental, (b) physical, or (c) neither.

We may ameliorate the task ahead of us by dealing with the first category very briefly. A mental monist believes the only reality to be ultimately mental, and the physical world to consist only of *ideas* in the mind. For this reason, the mental form of monism is usually called *idealism*. The earliest of the idealists we need mention is George Berkeley (1685-1753), an (Anglican) Irish bishop who, beginning from *empiricist* principles (i.e. from a theory which puts *experience* prior to all else), developed a view according to which things only exist insofar as they are perceived by an observer. A theory which conforms in part with Berkeley's is that of J.G. Fichte (1762-1814), one of the German idealists; for Fichte, however, it is the 'moral will' which is the ultimate reality and which creates its own objects. The culmination of German idealism comes with G.W.F. Hegel (1770-1831). Hegel's views are many and complex, and it will suffice here to say that, for Hegel, what is ultimately real is the Absolute, or divine Idea.

This does not pretend to be a full, or even an adequate, treatment of idealist approaches to the mind-body problem. Its purpose is merely to reveal why we do not need to concern ourselves with idealism here. For one thing, there are very few people today who take idealism seriously; a better reason for leaving it aside, however, is that it is irrelevant to our central purpose. This purpose is to throw light on the relation between minds and machines. Now if the idealist were correct, the answer to our question would be trivial and uninteresting: machines would be no more than ideas in the mind, like everything else. This does not, of course, mean that idealism is wrong, but simply that anyone who is seriously wedded to idealism may as well stop reading at this point. After this clarification, we will begin by looking at the position which stands at the opposite extreme to idealism – materialism.

the materialism of Armstrong and Smart

Two modern philosophers who take the extreme position of actually *identifying* the mental with the physical, are D.M. Armstrong and J.J.C. Smart. The essence of Armstrong's thesis is simple, though his defence of it is not. He believes that mental states simply *are* physical states of the organism's central nervous system. His definition of a mental state is in terms of its typical causes (stimuli) and effects (behaviour of the organism). He then presents the hypothesis that these causes and effects are 'contingently identical' with states of the central nervous system. For this reason, the kind of materialism propounded by Armstrong and Smart is often called Central State Materialism, though it is also known as Eliminative Materialism and the Mind-Body Identity Theory. To say that A is *contingently* identical with B, is to say that A is *in fact* one and the same with B, though it *might not have been*, i.e. it is not a logical truth that it is. In other words, Armstrong wants to regard it as a scientific discovery, and not just a matter of conceptual reasoning, that states of mind and states of the central nervous system are identical. What makes this thesis materialist is that he also regards the physical side of the equation as the more fundamental, and as that in terms of which the mental side is to be explained. This account is normally referred to as *reductivist*. Any theory is reductivist if it takes one kind of thing and 'reduces' it to another; that is, if it attempts to show that it is 'really no more than' the latter. Materialism in this way attempts to reduce the mental to the physical.

The problem for the materialist is to show how the apparently mental states or events such as the 'feels' and 'sensations' which we have seen earlier, can *really* be physical states of the organism. How, for example, is she to explain the apparently irreducible fact that a particular object *looks* the way it does to me, that there is something it is *like* to be me in this instance, to adopt Nagel's formulation discussed previously? Armstrong's answer is to identify perception with the acquisition, or possible acquistion, of beliefs about the world including our own bodies; and subsequently to give a *behavioural* account of the beliefs – that is, to identify the beliefs with their behavioural manifestations.

For all its apparent simplicity, Armstrong's theory has turned out to be in many ways a rather confused one. For it never becomes clear what it is that is supposed to be being 'reduced' to the physical, if mental states are to be *defined* in the way Armstrong suggests. The confusion shows itself in the fact that Armstrong himself seems never to be sure whether the 'inner' mental states are a kind of myth or delusion on our part, or whether they are real enough, but properly to be explained in terms of the nervous system. If the former, then his own writing is vitiated by constant reference to them; and if the latter, then it is hard to see why their supposed identity with physical states shows the physical states to be the only 'real' ones – except, perhaps, by being causally prior to the mental ones, though even this gives us no reason to think the pain less real than the kick!

This dilemma is implicitly dealt with by Smart, who is concerned to answer a certain kind of objection to his form of Armstrong-type materialism. Suppose, he says, someone accepts his thesis that sensations simply *are* physical states, and yet sees no reason to deny that these physical states have *irreducibly mental properties*. His response to this challenge is to treat the concepts which are claimed to be irreducibly mental (sensation concepts, etc.) in a way which involves no commitment to their being either mental or physical concepts. This analysis of them he calls a 'topic-neutral analysis'. In outline, what he suggests is that they be understood in terms of the 'inputs' and 'outputs' of the states in question. The concept of pain is not to be thought of as being about an 'inner' mental sensation, but rather in terms of typical stimulus (damage to body tissue, stimulation of nerves and so on), and typical response (crying out, rubbing the affected part, and suchlike). This refinement will not be discussed further just here, since it has something in common with both behaviourism, which will be dealt with in the next section, and with functionalism, which will be treated in the one following.

behaviourism: Watson, Skinner and Ryle

Behaviourism is a kind of theory which began life as a revolutionary methodology in psychology. Its founder was the American psychologist J.B. Watson, who first laid down its principles in a paper published in 1913, since when it has enjoyed much influence, even with many who would not go so far as to call themselves behaviourists. As a psychological methodology, behaviourism involves concentrating on the outward and observable behaviour of an organism, whilst attaching little importance to its own feelings and sensations. This elevation of the public and verifiable, whilst devaluing the mental and subjective, was held by many psychologists to place psychology on a more objective and scientific footing than that provided, for example, by introspection (observation of one's own mind). These behaviourists did not altogether deny the existence of introspectable sensations and feelings; they merely believed that from a scientific point of view they could safely drop out of the picture (cf. the views of Wittgenstein and Rorty, discussed earlier, on the mental 'dropping out' of the picture).

How, if these items are allowed to exist, can they possibly be ignored by psychologists, of all people? The answer lies in the *stimulus-response* explanation of human behaviour.

According to the behaviourist, human action has causes, and these causes are themselves outward and physical. For example, suppose we want to make an animal in a laboratory eat a certain kind of food which it is reluctant to eat. One thing we may do is to deprive it of other food until it becomes hungry and will eat what is available. Here we have a chain of events

deprivation ------> hunger ------> eating

which seems to be causally linked: the deprivation causes the hunger, and the hunger subsequently causes the eating. But if this is the case, given that the relation of causality is transitive, we can ignore the inner, unsurveyable hunger, and talk as though the deprivation directly causes the eating.

Behaviourists have since developed sophisticated theories and concepts to do with the nature and variety of conditioning. An example is the notion of 'operant conditioning', which is the kind of conditioning that requires the experimental subject to perform some task, such as pressing a lever, before receiving a reward. A well-known instrument of operant conditioning is the Skinner Box, a device used by the American psychologist B.F. Skinner (b.1904). Skinner, besides doing experimental research in psychology, has also conducted a campaign in recent years to defend behaviourism from its critics. In this way, he has become probably the best-known present-day behaviourist. His works include a novel, *Walden Two*, in which Skinner tries to demonstrate, by using the example of a fictional society, how mankind could live in a happier and more rational way if we would only agree to accept the idea that we are governed by conditioning, and yield to the more beneficial forms of it instead of holding out for mistaken ideals such as 'liberty'. This is also the thesis of Skinner's philosophical work *Beyond Freedom and Dignity*.

From the above, it will be clear that there is plenty to object to in the behaviourist program, should we be inclined to do so. However, from the point of view of our present concerns, the significant facts are that, whilst some behaviourist psychologists simply considered that the mental aspects 'drop out' of the question, or can be ignored, certain of the more extreme exponents actually argued that, due to their lack of objectivity, they cannot be regarded as real items in the world at all. This view influenced a number of anti-mentalist philosophers, who also came to be known as behaviourists. The best-known of these has been the English philosopher Gilbert Ryle (1900-1976). Ryle, whilst perhaps not being entirely happy with the label 'behaviourist', accepted that it might 'harmlessly' be applied to him. He is certainly the leading exponent of philosophy in the behaviourist spirit, though his version of it is a good deal more sophisticated than some.

Ryle's chief single work, in which he expounds this view, is his book *The Concept of Mind* (1949). In some ways it is difficult to sum up Ryle's own theory of the mind, since most of the book is devoted to attacking the accounts with which he disagrees. These are, he argues, systematically connected, since they have in common a misleading assumption about the mind, which Ryle regards as so pervasive that he calls it 'the official doctrine'. The official doctrine is, roughly speaking, the tradition of mind-body dualism which comes down from Descartes. It maintains that a person has, or is, two things, a mind and a body, and that there are mental entities, events and processes just as there are physical ones. It is this doctrine, Ryle says, which has perpetuated what he refers to as 'the myth of the ghost in the machine' – the idea of the person as a physical, mechanical thing, but inhabited by a ghostly, spiritual agent.

Well, as Ryle freely admits, we all constantly use language which seems to embody the idea of the ghost in the machine, or something like it. We not only say things like 'in my own mind', and 'a feeling inside me', but a host of other concepts, such as desires, beliefs, motives, intentions, seem to refer to inner and (to others) unobservable items. How can Ryle account for this?

The chief method which he uses to render these concepts harmless, is the *dispositional analysis* of the terms in question. Rather than seeing these psychological words as referring to things which are private to the subject of them, he analyses them as referring to *dispositions* on the part of people to engage in certain kinds of outward behaviour. Thus to say that a person *believes* something is not to say that he has an unobservable mental state of belief, but that he will act in particular ways under given circumstances: the belief that it is raining outside can be cashed in terms of a disposition to take an umbrella, etc. Similarly, to say that someone has a *desire* for a drink is to say that he will take steps to get a drink if possible, will not refuse one when offered, will tend to head for the bar, and so on.

This brings us to Ryle's characterization of the 'official doctrine' as a *category mistake*. In order to see what a category mistake involves, consider the example which Ryle gives to illustrate the notion. A visitor to England is shown round Oxford University: he is shown the colleges, libraries, laboratories and playing-fields, and then he asks, 'But where is the University?' His mistake was a category mistake in that he thought the University was something of the same *type* as colleges, libraries, etc., instead of something made up of them. In the same way, Ryle thinks that philosophers and others have been mistaken in thinking of the mind as something different from, but of the same type as, the body, in the sense that it has been thought proper to say that people have a mind *and* a body. Rather, Ryle argues, the mind is something constructed out of observable bodily behaviour and the dispositions which it displays.

What, then, of the existence of feelings and sensations, that chief bastion of the mentalist? Surely we cannot settle for a dispositional account of these, for are they not *par excellence* the mental items which are inaccesible to all but the person possessing them? To this, Ryle replies that the talk about such things is a product of the way in which language has been misused by mentalistic philosophers. What I observe at first hand, he says, are ordinary public objects in the world, not my own sensations or feelings. Like Watson, he seeks no reason to bring in a private, mental entity to stand between the physical stimulus and the physical response. Indeed he claims that, if we understood the issue properly:

> We have no employment for such expressions as 'objects of sense', 'sensible object', 'sensum', 'sense datum', 'sense content', 'sense field' and 'sensibilia'... They commemorate nothing more than the attempt to give the concepts of sensation the jobs of concepts of observation, an attempt which inexorably ended in the postulation of sense data as counterparts of the common objects of observation. It also follows that we need no private stages for these postulated extra objects, nor puzzle our heads to describe the indescribable relations between these postulated entities and everyday things.

Now in some respects, Ryle has been clearly recognized as correct. 'Sense data', the supposed *immediate* objects of perception (which might or might not correspond to real objects in the world) cannot be discussed and described in the way that public, physical objects can, for we have no public language in which to discuss them (remember Wittgenstein and the Private Language Argument). Nor should they be spoken of as though they were extra objects in the world, alongside the public and physical ones. Yet none of this alters the fact that there is such a thing as *the way in which things appear* to a person: there is *something it is like* to be him when observing a particular object, over and above what can be reported of him by another observer. The fact that this is so, and that we have no common language for talking of our private sensations, is the reason why we cannot make headway with such questions as 'Do other people see colours the way I see them?' Nor, despite what some philosophers have said, does there seem to be good reason for thinking this is not a proper question.

Here, Ryle seems to waver, for he sometimes seems to be denying this, and sometimes not. As the philosopher Stuart Hampshire has put it:

> ...Ryle has not decided whether he is saying (a) that no mental concepts 'stand for' imperceptible (=ghostly) processes or states: all 'designate' some perceptible or nearly perceptible (e.g. 'silent colliloquies) patterns of behaviour: or less drastically (b) that all statements involving mental concepts are in principle testable, directly or indirectly and in various degrees, by observation of the behaviour of the persons concerned.

It seems we must conclude that if what he is saying is the latter, then his method has not entirely succeeded in exorcising the 'ghost in the machine', and that if it is the former, then more argument is surely necessary. For how, on any ordinary understanding, can we actually *equate*, for example, the belief that it is raining with the disposition to carry an umbrella? Even if we make the disposition more sophisticated, including also such things as wearing a hat, saying 'It's raining' and so on, there is still a logical gap between the behaviour and the belief; is it not still possible (as some people have suggested) that the person in question is a 'perfect actor' who, for reasons of his own, wants us to *think* he believes it is raining? The behaviourist can, perhaps, elaborate his account of the disposition even further, including the proviso that the person should not be intending to deceive, where the notion of *intending* is likewise cashed out in dispositional terms. Yet there seems to be more than a whiff of circularity about this. Furthermore, it is unlikely to satisfy us when it comes to feels and sensations: no amount of outward behaviour and dispositions is going to add up to a pain, to the pain *itself*. We will now move on, as promised, to consider an account of the mind which has links with both materialism and behaviourism: functionalism.

functionalism and Turing machines

A currently popular, though not always well-understood, approach to the philosophy of mind is known as functionalism. The best way to go about understanding the family of views which come under this heading, is by considering some criticisms of materialism and behaviourism, both of which sets of criticism helped to give rise to the acceptance of functionalism. What makes some people hesitate before accepting a straightforwardly materialist position is the following consideration. It seems very unlikely that the physical state of the brain or whatever, which corresponds to, say, pain in a human being, is exactly the same physical state which corresponds to pain in another animal such as a squirrel. Thus to say that to be in pain *is* to be in this physical state begins to look implausible. What deters many people from accepting a behaviourist position, is their recognition that the inputs and outputs of mental states need not be always physical states – they might be themselves mental states. Worry gives rise to depression, and not just to nail-biting. Functionalism, at least on first sight, promises to remedy both of these difficulties.

According to the functionalist, mental states are functional states. That is to say, if an organism is in a given mental state, this state can be defined in terms of its causal roles. Thus the state of feeling thirst is that feature which is characterized by being caused by dehydration, and by causing the action of drinking. This is what thirst in one creature, or kind of creature, has in common with thirst in another, which makes them both cases of thirst and not something else (hence apparently overcoming the objection to materialism). Furthermore, we can say that thirst may cause not only drinking, which is a physical thing, but also, for example, thoughts of water, which are mental (thus seemingly solving one of the problems about behaviourism, which is that a single 'mental state' does not always have only physical inputs and outputs). Some functionalists trace the origin of this view back to Aristotle, though in the form which it now takes it is relatively recent.

It is interesting for our purposes that a quite popular form of functionalism involves comparing the mental states of an organism to the states of a machine. The most common machine version of functionalism is called Turing Machine Functionalism. A Turing machine is the simplest kind of computational machine, and is named after its inventor Alan Turing, whom we came across in chapter 5. A Turing machine is a *theoretical machine* in the sense that we don't need physically to build the machine in order to reap the benefits of the concept of such a machine, for its purpose is itself essentially theoretical. The original set of problems which the Turing machine idea was meant to illuminate were to do with the notion of calculability in general, and the usefulness of the Turing machine idea lay in the fact that it allows us to reduce all methods of calculation to a single, basic, underlying set of operations. A Turing machine may be thought of as having a number of *machine states*, and as reading symbols from squares along an endless tape. Some of the squares may be blank. The basic operations are performed by the machine in response to the combination of (a) the machine state it is in, and (b) the symbol it is reading in the current square. The *table* for the machine is what tells it what to do in a given situation, rather like the program of an ordinary computer. A machine table may look something like this:

    S1, 1, R, S2
    S1, 2, R, S3
    S2, 1, R, S3
    S2, 2, 3, S2
    S2, 3, R, S1
    S3, 1, 3, S3
    S3, 2, 4, S3
    S3, 3, R, S1
    S3, 4, R, S1

The first line says that if the machine is in state S1 and is reading a 1, then it is to move one square to the right and go to state S2. The second line says that if the machine is in state S1 and is reading a 2, then it is to move a square to the right and go into state S3. The third line tells us that if it is in state S2 and is reading a 1, then it must move right a square and go into state S3. The fourth line says that if it finds itself in S2 and reading a 2, it is to print a 3 (erasing the 2) and remain in S2. The meaning of the remaining lines should be obvious. To illustrate the idea, let us take the fifth line and show how the machine deals with it.

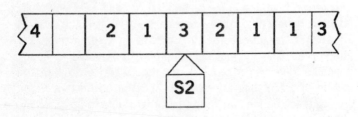

Figure 1

Figure 1 shows the situation just *before* the action has taken place. The machine is in state S2 (as indicated under the triangular head which 'reads' the tape), and is confronted with a 3 on the tape.

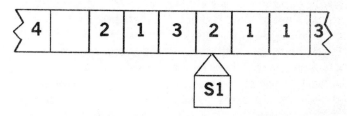

Figure 2

In Figure 2, we see how things look *after* the machine has obeyed the instruction. Having found itself in state S2 and scanning a 3, it has moved one square to the right and gone into state S1. (As an exercise, work out from the table what it will do *next*.) These two figures show what would be happening

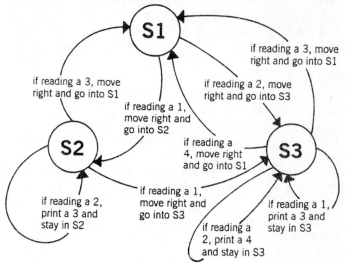

Figure 3

with the Turing machine if we actually built such a machine. A more abstract diagram, however, will allow us to depict the whole repertoire of the machine, i.e. all the actions prescribed by the nine instructions in the table. This is given in Figure 3.

After all this, it might be reasonable to ask: what is all this *for*? What good is a theoretical machine which obeys an abstract set of rules laid out in a mathematical table? To begin to answer this, let us consider one, among many, of the things which this abstract specification of a machine may be taken to represent. Imagine a machine which dispenses cups of tea at a price of 15 pence per cup, and which accepts either 5 pence or 10 pence pieces. Whilst nobody is using the machine, it remains in its 'waiting state'. Let us take this to be state S1 in Figure 3. Now let the insertion of 5 pence correspond to reading a 1, and the insertion of 10 pence to reading a 2. It will be seen that on receiving 5 pence the machine moves to the right, which might be regarded as equivalent to 'waiting for the next coin', and goes into state S2, which therefore corresponds to 'waiting for 10 pence'. If, however, the machine receives 10 pence, it moves right and goes into state S3, which can be seen as 'waiting for 5 pence'. Now if it is in state S2 (waiting for 10 pence) and it receives a 5, then it moves right (waiting for the next coin) and goes into state S3, i.e. waiting for 5 pence. If, on the other hand, it is in state S2 and receives 10 pence, it prints a 3 (which we may interpret as dispensing a cup of tea) and remains in S2, whereupon it moves right and goes into S1, waiting for things to start all over again. If it is in S3 and receives a 5, it likewise prints a 3 (gives a cup of tea), stays in S3, and subsequently moves right and goes back into S1. But if it is in S3 and receives 10 pence, it has 5 pence too much; it therefore prints a 4 (corresponding to the action of dispensing-a-tea-and-giving-5 pence-change) and remains in S3, after which it moves right and goes back to S1, waiting for the process to start again. The tea machine described above therefore *instantiates* the Turing machine whose table was given above.

Now what the Turing machine functionalist suggests is that mental states can be seen as like the states (S1, S2 and S3 in the above example) of the theoretical machine. It will not then matter *how* the states are in fact instantiated (what the states physically *are*) – the same states can have different physical instantiations in different types of creature. For example, thirst in a camel will go along with a different physical state from thirst in a human being. What they have in common, however, which makes them both cases of thirst, is that they occupy the same role in the system; in the same way that what counts as a tea machine of the above kind being in state S3 is its relations with states S1 and S2. What that state *is*, is characterized by when and how it derives from S2 and results in S1 (or in remaining in the same state S3). Thus we may *build* the machine in electronic, hydraulic, steam-driven, or any other form: but what makes all cases of S3 cases of S3 is the functional role they perform – their causal relations with other states in the machine, including inputs and outputs. So whilst the materialist says that what all cases of thirst have in common is the physical thing, and the behaviourist claims that what they have in common is a behavioural feature, the functionalist says that the feature they have in common is *functional* – a common causal role. And the machine version of functionalism holds that this can be described in terms of a table for a theoretical machine such as the Turing machine.

the varieties of functionalism
Unfortunately, not all functionalists agree on what follows from this. Some functionalists are also materialists, and think that functionalism supports materialism (Armstrong and Smart, for instance, both agree with a certain version of functionalism). Others believe that functionalism entails the *falsity* of materialism. For example, David Lewis, who is on the side of Smart and Armstrong, argues that since it is in fact a physical state in all known cases which occupies the causal role corresponding to a functional state such as 'pain', the functional view must lead us to believe that pains are physical things. On the other hand, the non-materialist functionalists such as Jerry Fodor and Hilary Putnam point to the fact that the occupant of that causal role *need not necessarily* be physical: at least it

does not follow from the principles of functionalism as such, that it has to be. They stop short of *identifying* each functional state with a physical state, and regard the functional state as merely that which all pains, for example, have in common, which makes them pains rather than something else.

When someone claims that all instances of functional state such-and-such are in fact physical states with common physical characteristics (e.g. that every individual pain is a physical state with the same properties), he is known as a *token identity theorist* – a 'token' being an 'instance'. On the other hand, when a person holds merely that pain in general is physical though its embodiment may be different in different creatures, he is said to be a *type identity theorist*, which in a sense is a weaker position – he claims only to explain what type of thing pain is, and not what each individual pain is.

The fact that functionalism allows us, as we saw above, to characterize mental states in terms of other mental states does not, therefore, mean that the functionalist has to accept mental states as ineliminable. All it means is that we cannot eliminate mental states one at a time. That is, we cannot give a reductive analysis of a single, isolated mental state; otherwise we end up being unable to give an account of some others. For example, if 'thirst' is typified by the fact that it gives rise to 'thoughts of water', then the 'thoughts of water' cannot be explained away, they cannot be eliminated, without making the concept of thirst unintelligible. A move which the functionalist can make, however, is to claim that mental states as a whole are eliminable; that is, that they are eliminable provided we eliminate them *all at once*. Thus, we cannot eliminate them singly by saying 'Mental state such-and-such is really only something-or-other', but we can do it by saying 'Mental states in general are really only this-that-and-the-other'. This leaves room for the functionalist to be also a materialist. But at the same time it leaves it open for the non-materialist to embrace functionalism. The fact is, that the materialist and non-materialist functionalists tend to understand functionalism in different ways. The materialists take themselves to be talking about actual states which occupy particular functional roles, whilst the non-materialists understand themselves as only saying something about what it is to be a state of a particular type.

This ambiguity helps us to show up how functionalism falls short of doing the job which we hoped it might do − of elucidating the connection between mental and physical states. For functionalism, broadly understood, is compatible with too many different points of view concerning this relation. In some of its forms, it is merely a version of Central State Materialism; in other forms, it is so non-committal about what *actual* mental states are, that it sidesteps the central question in which we are interested. For the broad-minded functionalist, the same causal role could, in principle, be filled by a physical state, an irreducibly mental state or 'spiritual' state, or indeed by some other kind of state of which we have no conception.

Despite the apparently promising connection, then, which some functionalists draw between human thinking and machine behaviour, it turns out that the merely theoretical character of the machine in question (its independence of any specific implementation) deprives it of the explanatory power which it appeared at first sight to possess.

Now before going on to discuss less extreme forms of monism, we will consider a relatively modern defence of the doctrine of materialism, but one which is essentially different from the kinds outlined above.

Davidson's anomalous monism

This mysterious-sounding theory is, in fact, a version of materialism, though not along the lines which we have seen earlier. It was propounded by the American philosopher Donald Davidson in an article published in 1970. Davidson's reasoning differs from that of, say, Armstrong and Smart, not so much in its conclusion as in its starting point. A typical materialist is likely to have, as one of his reasons for being a materialist, the fact that he believes there to be law-like correlations between certain physical events and certain events of the sort commonly called mental. For example, he will regard it is a 'law of nature' that when a particular event occurs in the brain, a given 'mental state' will be present in the person whose brain it is. Davidson's case depends, however, on the alleged *absence* of psycho-physical laws. Our correlation of mental and physical happen-ings is, he says, only a matter of rough generalization:

> ...if an event of a certain mental sort has usually been accompanied by an event of a certain physical sort, this often is a good reason to expect other cases to follow suit...The generalizations that embody such practical wisdom are assumed to be only roughly true, or they are explicitly stated in probabilistic terms, or they are insulated from counterexamples by generous escape clauses. Their importance lies mainly in the support they lend singular causal claims and related explan-ations of particular events. The support derives from the fact that such a generalization, however crude and vague, may provide good reason to believe that underlying the particular case there is a regularity that could be formulated sharply and without caveat.

What sort of regularity? Well, Davidson agrees, mental events are at least sometimes the causes and effects of physical events. And if two things are connected as cause and event, then this causal relation must be an instance of a *law*. But since there are no laws connecting mental and physical events, one of these must be reducible to the other, in order that we can preserve the idea of causal interaction. The one which must be reduced, Davidson argues, is the mental, since it does not constitute a 'closed system', whereas the physical does. What this means is that we can, in principle, find a physical cause for every physical event (there may also appear to be a mental one, but there will at least be some physical cause – a brain event perhaps); but we cannot find a mental cause for every mental event (the cause of a pain, for example, is usually a physical cause, and there is often no further mental event which causes *it*).

Two things should make us wary of accepting this position too readily. First, how seriously should we take the fact that detailed psycho-physical laws seem not to be forthcoming? Might it not simply be that establishing the appropriate correlations is too difficult owing to the enormous open-ended variety of physical and mental behaviour, when compared with the behaviour of inanimate objects? And why, anyway, is

Davidson so certain that every physical event can be ascribed a physical cause? It cannot be shown from experience, any more than can psychophysical correlations, and what is more, many modern quantum physicists actually reject it!

The second objection is more subtle, and concerns the fact that, if Davidson is right, some events will have both a physical and a mental *description* though they will 'really' be physical events. Now since, according to him, physical events all stand in causal relations, and therefore instantiate laws, and since he thinks mental events *don't* stand in law-like relations with physical ones, it follows that on his view some events are instances of a law under one description but not under another. But his starting-point was that mental events are sometimes causes and effects of physical ones. Yet his own theory dictates that mental events can be causes of physical ones only under their physical description, whereas it is fairly clear that the initial premise is attractive only if it is the *mental* descriptions of these events which is in question. We are surely more certain that stubbing your toe causes the feeling of pain, than we are that it causes such-and-such a brain state.

In the next chapter we will be looking at some other forms of monism, and also asking where the present part of the discussion is leading as regards our central topic.

8: more about monism

The monist-type positions which we glanced at in the last chapter were largely of a materialist or functionalist kind. Continuing to explore the many permutations of monism, we will at this point leave all forms of materialism and functionalism behind, and first of all look at a philosophical position which takes its starting point from a very different angle.

Strawson and the concept of a person

This is the view laid out in Peter Strawson's book *Individuals* (1959). Strawson's approach to the mind-body problem differs radically from any that we have looked at so far, in that he adopts the idea of a *person* as the central, primitive notion, rather than that of either mind or body as such. Once we have the concept of a person we can, according to Strawson, then go on to attribute mental as well as physical properties to persons. But it is first of all essential to our concept of a person that persons should be the kind of thing we can identify and reidentify. We must, in other words, be able to tell, in principle, which person is which: to tell one person from another, and be able to recognize a person as being the same from one occasion to another. This is because our concept of a person is a concept of an *individual* thing and not, for example, of a property or of a substance. Now minds, conceived of as purely immaterial, or abstract, things, are *not* such that they can be reidentified in this sense: if people *only* had minds, we would be literally unable to distinguish one person from another. It is the physical body which makes reidentification possible, and which therefore serves as the 'anchor' for our concept of a person. In Strawson's words:

> The concept of a person is logically prior to that of an individual consciousness. The concept of a person is not to be analysed as that of an animated body or an embodied anima. This is not to say that the concept of a pure individual consciousness might not have a logically secondary existence, if one thinks, or finds, it desirable. We speak of a dead person – a body – and in the same secondary way we might at least think of a disembodied person. A person is not an embodied ego, but an ego might be a disembodied person, retaining the logical benefit of individuality from having been a person.

Strawson goes even further, however, and claims that the possibility of attributing mental properties to ourselves depends on our being prepared, at least sometimes, to attribute them to other people. It will be noticed that this is an inversion of the traditional way of approaching the problem of other minds (which we discussed in chapters 2 and 3). It perhaps has more in common with the philosophy of Wittgenstein, in this respect, than have most other accounts. The traditional approach takes as primary the ability to attribute mental states to ourselves, and regards the possibility of attributing them to others as depending on it. Strawson, however, argues that since it was outward bodily behaviour which provides the anchor for our concept of a person, and therefore for our concept of a mind, it is by observing others that we acquire the concept, and not from observing ourselves. I don't actually *observe* my own behaviour, though I might be *aware* of it: I am the agent, and not a spectator. Only then, on Strawson's view, are we able to attribute mental properties to ourselves. He says:

> If, in identifying the things to which states of consciousness are to be ascribed, private experiences are to be all one has to go on, then, just for the very same reason as that for which there is, from one's own point of view, no question of telling that a private experience is one's own, there is also no telling that a private experience is another's...One can ascribe states of consciousness to oneself only if one can ascribe them to others. One can ascribe them to others only if one can identify other subjects of experience. And one cannot identify others if one can identify them *only* as subjects of experience, possessors of

states of consciousness.

The result of all this is an account of the relation between mind and body, according to which they are such that there is just one kind of thing – a person – to which *both* physical and mental properties are applicable, though persons are reidentified through the reidentification of their bodies, which is to give some precedence to the physical over the mental concepts.

It is perhaps difficult to tell, in forming an opinion of Strawson's view, whether he is standing the traditional problem of other minds on its head, or whether he is putting it back on its feet after its having been turned upside-down by earlier philosophers. One trouble with the Strawsonian account is that the reasons given for it do not really add up to a logically strict defence. He says that the mental cannot consist merely of private experiences, which is precisely what most people *do* think the mental consists of, since, if 'private experiences are all one has to go on', we would be unable in all cases to say *whose* experience the experience was. But to say that private experiences are what mental things *are*, is not the same as to say that private experiences are 'all we have to go on'. As we saw in earlier chapters, it is quite possible to believe in private, inner experiences, which nonetheless have public and outward *symptoms*. To point out that we could not form the *concept* of mind if we did not have other people's outward behaviour to go on, does not actually imply anything at all about the nature of mind *itself*. The nature of the thing which the word 'mind' refers to, if it does refer to a thing at all, is not guaranteed to be exhausted by the nature of those things by which we originally learned how to use the word. And it is with the nature of the mental itself with which we are concerned.

Of course, Strawson does not go so far as to deny that there is *any* 'inner' experience. The problem is, that he does not really give us an account of *its* relation to the physical world: to say that there is just one kind of thing to which both mental and physical properties are attributable, and that mental concepts are learned through observing physical behaviour, does not by any means add up to a theory of the relation between the mental and the physical.

It is, however, a move in a certain direction, and that is the direction in which we are going. For one aspect of Strawson's view is that it displaces both mind and matter from the centre of the stage, in favour of a concept which is neither exactly mental nor physical. Now at the time when Strawson was writing there was already a theory in existence which went further in this direction – the theory known as 'neutral monism'. Its most famous exponent was Bertrand Russell, and it is to his account of it that we now turn.

Russell's neutral monism

The theory of neutral monism comes originally from the American psychologist William James (1842-1910). Russell adopted it during a significant period of his career though he took some time to be convinced of it, and later abandoned it. It is called 'neutral' for the reason that it neither makes the mental secondary to the physical, nor vice versa. Rather, the neutral monist sees all mental and physical things as *constructed* out of something more basic, but something which is in itself neither physical nor mental. Russell sums up the outlines of neutral monism very succinctly in a well-known passage, and we will let him speak for himself:

> 'Neutral monism' – as opposed to idealistic monism and materialistic monism – is the theory that things commonly regarded as mental and the things commonly regarded as physical do not differ in respect of any intrinsic property possessed by one set and not by the other, but differ only in respect of arrangement and context.

Russell illustrates this idea by comparison with a telephone directory which has both an alphabetical and a geographical listing, so that every name appears twice, but in a different order. He goes on:

> The affinities of a given thing are quite different in the two orders, and its causes and effects obey different laws. Two objects may be connected in the mental world by association of ideas, and in the physical world by the law of gravitation. The whole context of an object is so different in the mental order

from what it is in the physical order, that the object itself is thought to be duplicated, and in the mental order it is called an 'idea', namely the idea of the same object in the physical order. But this duplication is a mistake: 'ideas' of chairs and tables are identical with chairs and tables, but are considered in their mental context, not in the context of physics.

It is important to recognize how heavily Russell's form of neutral monism depended on the fact that he was also a *constructionist*: he held the principle that, wherever possible, we should 'substitute constructions out of known entities for inference to unknown entities'. In other words, he believed that we should accept as basic only those things with which we are so well acquainted that we are in no doubt about their existence and nature; and that we should try to show how the more obscure things which we talk about, can be 'constructed' out of the basic ones. To 'construct' B out of A, in this sense, means to show how B can be understood in terms of A; so that acquaintance with A will, once we know how the construction works, allow us to understand statements about B without any trouble. Now the way in which we apply the constructionist principle will depend on *what* we take to be the kind of thing with which we are fundamentally best acquainted – physical objects, our own ideas, or whatever.

Russell thought what any person is best acquainted with is his own sense experience. He therefore sets about showing how both physical and mental things can be constructed out of sense experience. Sense experience is, of course, the private and immediate experience of an individual person. It is significant that, in his later neutral monist period, Russell allowed that the ultimate stuff out of which everything else is constructed includes not only our *own* sense experience, but also the experiences which it is reasonable to suppose that other people would have had, if they had, for example, been in a given place at a given time.

There are, then, two categories of things which we need to construct from sense experience: physical objects and minds. Physical objects present little problem, granted Russell's starting points. Minds are slightly harder. Russell begins by explaining that the 'self' which each of us is inclined to attribute to himself, is elusive. That is to say, if I try to capture what it is that I mean by my 'self', if I try, as it were, to 'turn the spotlight on itself', I am unable to discover anything in my own experience which corresponds to it. If we ask 'What are supposed to be the contents of the mind, or components of the mind?', we may regard them as falling into two categories. Into one category fall such supposed mental states as desire, belief, intention and the emotions. Now there are plenty of people who claim that we can do away with these, as far as counting them as genuine mental *states* is concerned; for there is nothing discoverable in us which corresponds to them (they have no *phenomenology*, as we say). An analysis can, however, allegedly be given in terms of behaviour: a dispositional account along the lines of Ryle. The other category is more difficult though, for into it fall sensations, feels, images: those things which constiture *one's own experience of* the world, the way things are 'from the inside'. But this is surely 'sense experience' itself. This, then, is what the mind is constructed out of, and what it is supposed to comprise. This shows how 'mental' and 'physical' things, in Russell's words, 'differ only in respect of arrangement and context'.

Neutral monism has some very attractive aspects. It prevents those of us who cannot swallow dualism, from having to choose between mind and matter as the more 'real', the dominant partner. However, it also has its drawbacks. Firstly, the way in which Russell presents it rather makes it sound as though, besides mind and matter, there is also some 'neutral stuff' out of which they are both constructed. If this were the case, all we would be doing would be adding a third category to those of mental and physical, and aggravating the problem. This is not what Russell intends, however. When we look at what it is that both the mental and the physical are constructed out of, on his account, we find that it is the very kind of thing which normally characterizes the mental: sense experience. For what else can 'sense experience' mean but things *as experienced*? In other words, our experiences themselves: our feels, sensations, call them what you like. In the next section, we will look at a view of mind and matter which has a great deal in common with Russell's, though perhaps it commits us to rather less.

double aspect theories

Those accounts of the mind-body relationship which are known as 'double aspect theories' trace their ancestry at least back to the Jewish Dutch philosopher Baruch (or Benedict) Spinoza (1632-77). Reacting against the dualism of Descartes, which we discussed in the last chapter, Spinoza thought it impossible that two substances as different as Cartesian mind and matter could interact with each other. For reasons of his own, which by no means all of us would wish to accept, Spinoza also thought that there could only ultimately be *one* substance. According to Spinoza this could be seen as Nature taken as a whole, or as God in whom everything exists. Having rejected the dualism of God and Nature, it was a reasonable step to reject the dualism of mind and matter. Yet once again Spinoza wishes to do justice to both, for he understands the claims of both. Thus he was led to a monism which came down neither on the side of mind nor of matter: a double aspect theory. Now a double aspect theory is one which holds that the mind and body of a person are two aspects of a single underlying reality, distinguishable from each other, but inseparable. As Spinoza himself expresses it, 'thinking substance and extended substance are one and the same substance, comprehended now through one attribute, now through the other'. Something of the same flavour as Russell's account comes across very strongly here.

But what is especially attractive about a double aspect theory is that it allows us to reject both the extremes of materialism and idealism whilst neither committing us to some third thing, nor threatening to collapse into idealism. Unlike Russell's neutral monism, a double aspect theory need not lead us, on the other hand, to postulate some neutral stuff out of which both mind and matter are constructed, nor, on the other, to regard the stuff out of which they are constructed as being mental stuff (which Russell comes perilously close to doing, though he does not wish to do it). The double aspect theorist need accept nothing more than the two aspects themselves. And if anyone says 'aspects of *what* – anything called an aspect must be an aspect *of* something', the double aspect theorist can claim that what there is to know about a thing is exhausted by the sum total of its aspects, and in particular that what there is to be known about persons is exhausted by their physical and mental aspects.

This is not meant to be a thoroughgoing defence of, or even elucidation of, double aspect theories. There is a great deal more to be said about this kind of view, and a great many varieties which such an account might take. This is intended only to make the point that the double aspect approach seems to be another step in the right direction, with regard to the way the exposition in this chapter has been developing. For it allows its adherents to reject the simple choice between mind and matter. No theory which forces us to make this false choice is going to do full justice to either. Although there are modern double aspect theorists, Spinoza remains the best known. Thus we seem at this point to have come, chronologically at least, full circle: for we began our look at the question of minds and bodies at the beginning of chapter 6 with Descartes, an older contemporary of Spinoza. But there is still one more kind of view to consider in the development of this exposition – that of Kant. The fact that it has been left until this point may be seen as reflecting both the way it fits into the structure of our argument, and also this author's sympathy with the Kantian position in general.

Kant and transcendental idealism
In some of what has gone before in this book, we have in fact been skirting around certain aspects of the Kantian philosophy without actually meeting it head-on; though the reader without much prior philosophical knowledge is unlikely to have recognised it. At the end of chapter 4 it was mentioned that Kant was the first person explicitly to identify certain arguments as transcendental arguments, a transcendental argument being an argument which begins from the facts as we know them to be,

and proceeds to draw conclusions about what must further be the case in order for these facts to be possible. And earlier in this chapter we looked at the approach to the mind-body problem adopted by Strawson, whose own metaphysical views are derived partly from a certain understanding of the doctrines of Kant.

Immanuel Kant (1724-1804) lived his entire life in and around the University of Konigsberg, then in Germany, now the USSR. Kant is arguably the greatest philosopher of the modern period, sometimes being said to have synthesised and harmonised the major traditions of rationalism and empiricism which were current in the eighteenth century. As with most great and prolific writers, Kant's writings are not always easy to interpret, and it must be borne in mind that not everyone would agree with everything which will be said in the following sketch of his views which relate to the present topic. What is offered here can, however, be seen as a fairly orthodox account.

The Kantian approach to our subject must of necessity be approached a little obliquely, for Kant himself does not talk in terms of mind and bodies, much less of a 'mind-body problem' as such. Here the influence of Kant on Strawson is apparent in retrospect. The general metaphysical position held by Kant in his mature writings is known as transcendental idealism, a label coined by Kant himself. This position involves, initially, making a distinction between *things as they appear to us*, and *things as they are in themselves*.

This distinction is not as straightforward as it might appear on first sight. It is not simply that we are sometimes mistaken about the way things really are, as in thinking that something is green and discovering on closer inspection that it is blue. Rather, the way things appear to us, for Kant, is all that we can possibly know about them. Appearances which turn out to be in the ordinary sense untrue to reality, can be corrected only by reference to further appearances. The thing as it really is, however, can never be known to us at all, for the purely logical reason that all our experiences comes to us through the medium of our own faculties – sense organs, nervous system, and so on. A creature with a different sort of make-up (one of Nagel's bats, perhaps!) would experience the same object very differently, maybe not even by means of sight, sound, etc., at all.

If, then, there is a 'real' object underlying, and giving rise to, all the possible ways of experiencing it, then this 'object as it is in itself' must be independent of, or neutral between, all of these ways in which it presents itself to different kinds of percipients. And Kant believes that there must indeed be a 'real' object underlying the appearances. According to Kant, there can be no appearances without there being something *of which* they are appearances. Kant refers to the realm of appearances, or things as they appear, as the *phenomenal* world, and to that of things as they actually are in themselves as the *noumenal* world. It must not be thought, however, that Kant literally believed in two 'worlds': the phenomenal world is merely the noumenal world as it appears to us. And about this noumenal world nothing can be said, except that it must be postulated as necessary to explain the existence of the appearances, which is why the argument here is a transcendental one.

Where, then, do minds fit into this picture? Do they belong to the world of appearances or that of things as they are in themselves? If we have been following the argument so far, it will probably be clear that the answer is: neither wholly one nor wholly the other, since everything we are aware of has *both* aspects to it. Yet any given person only directly experiences one mind – his own. Nor (and this is crucially important) does a person even have experience of his own mind as it is in itself. In this respect, even one's own mind, insofar as one can know it, is just part of the world of experience, the phenomenal world. Thus Kant talks usually about the experience of one's own *self*, rather than of one's mind, lumping together everything a person can know about himself as phenomenal, as opposed to the noumenal self about which nothing can be known at all. (When what Kant has in mind is the traditional mind-body distinction he sometimes talks of 'inner' versus 'outer' experience.)

Yet although nothing can be known of the noumenal self, Kant regards it as indispensable if we care to make proper sense of things, just as he regards all other noumenal objects as indispensable. The chief reason for this is also based on a transcendental argument: for any experience to be possible, there has to be a subject which experiences as well as an object which is experienced. And the phenomenal self, being by definition an appearance, will not fill this role. Kant has two further arguments besides this for the concept of the noumenal self. One is based on the need to explain free will and moral judgement, but we will avoid going into this side of his work here. The other is rather obscure, and involves the claim that the existence, though not of course the nature, of this noumenal self accompanies all our experience, in the form of one's awareness of oneself as the subject of it.

Nothing, then, may be said about the noumenal self, except that it must exist, and possibly that it must be thought of as simple and indivisible, since it is what integrates and 'pulls together' all my perceptions, forming them into a unity – which is why my experiences, according to Kant, are able to present themselves as the experiences of the same person, rather than being mutually independent, disjointed and disembodied. We are now faced with two distinctions rather than the traditional one. For the phenomenal self is obviously closely related to the noumenal self, and stands with it over against the 'external world'; yet it stands with the external world, and over against the noumenal self, in that it is phenomenal, in common with everything else which can be experienced. The position seems, in other words, to be as follows:

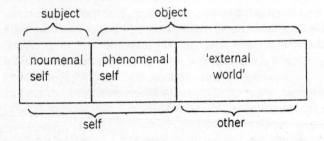

Figure 4

If we have understood the central ideas in the foregoing, we may now ask: what advantages, if any, does the Kantian position have over rival views, apart from the compelling force of Kant's arguments themselves? And how can it be of help to us here? Firstly, some of the unclarity of the physical-mental distinction are removed if we replace talk of mind and body with talk of subject and object – the thing which experiences and the thing experienced. Secondly, and partly as a result of this, we are able to retain the most useful insight of the double aspect type of theory, seen in the last section, whilst overcoming its greatest drawback.

To elaborate on this: the most attractive feature of the double aspect approach, as we noticed earlier, is the fact that it saves us from having to make a false choice between 'physical' and 'mental' and 'reducing' one of these to the other in such a way that only one of them turns out to be ultimately real. What we want is to be able to regard the mental and the physical as each possessing its own kind of reality. The drawback with a simple double aspect view, however, is that we are unable to answer the question 'Aspects of *what*?', for what we are left with is nothing but 'aspects', a position which Kant, at least, regards as untenable.

The way in which the Kantian approach can help us out of the dilemma is, perhaps, roughly as follows. By making the distinction between self and other cut across the distinction between subject and object, Kant shows, in effect, how we can retain the insight that the mental and the physical are somehow complementary rather than alternatives between which we have to choose, whilst at the same time allowing us to make a distinction between what is ultimately real and what is only appearance. For the wedge between self and other is driven in a different place from that between noumenal and phenomenal. Everything which can be an object of experience has, for Kant, a real, noumenal existence and also a corresponding appearance or appearances in the phenomenal world. This goes for ordinary physical objects. And since nothing can be said about the noumenal – about things as they are in themselves, the mental and the physical are, in this respect, on a par with each other: no question of choosing them arises. Of course, there exist other selves, besides what is, for me, the 'external world'. But they are all in the same position, and none is a part of the world of any other one – which ought to remind us of the reasons for which solipsism at first seemed inescapable in chapter 2. Kant's explanation of the necessity for other minds is different from Wittgenstein's, but is also based on transcendental arguments; we need not pursue it in detail here. It will suffice to say that Kant believes we must understand them by analogy with our own, but we should bear in mind that this is not the same thing as saying that we must *believe in them* because of any analogy with ourselves.

where do we go from here?
What bearing, then, does all this have on our main topic, that of the relationship between human mental life and the putative mentality of some machines? Firstly, the mind-body problem has to be taken seriously. If what we are after is a theory about the relation between the physical and mental aspects of machines, then this cannot be independent of some broader account of the relation between the mental and the physical in general. If, for example, we were central state materialists with regard to the human mind-body problem, this would give us a very different view of the conditions under which a machine could have a mental life, from that of a person who was convinced of the truth of Malbranche's occasionalism!

Secondly, it is hard to make convincing any view according to which either the mental or the physical aspect of a consciously thinking creature is 'really' only the other aspect under some different guise. In other words, it is hard to make either physical or mental reductionism plausible, since both appear to have features which are irreducible: the physical world seems to operate too independently of our wills and expectations for it to be 'all in the mind' (and in any case, whose mind, if we are not to be solipsists?); and the reality of the mental shows itself in the fact that no merely physical account of what is going on seems to add up to a description of the mental life as we experience it – any such physical account would be logically compatible with there being 'nobody at home', no consciousness present, at all.

Finally, it does seem that there exist ways of accounting for both mental and physical aspects of a thinking thing, without necessarily doing away with the distinction between what is ultimately real and what is secondary or merely apparent, though as we have seen, such an account is not going to be simple – and why should we expect it to be? If we are on the right lines in pursuing something like a Kantian approach to this issue, then we seem bound to accept this: that to be really consciously thinking is to have a viewpoint on the world, the nature of which is determined by the nature of one's own make-up. To be a subject, to have such a viewpoint, is to have a *particular* viewpoint, the nature of which is determined by the way in which one is able to experience. This fits in well with the earlier point, that the question 'Is this thing consciously thinking?' is the same as to ask 'Is there an answer to the question: what is it like to be this thing?' And, even if the argument from analogy for other minds will not suffice to guarantee their existence, yet if we are to accept other minds at all, we must understand them by analogy with our own, which gives us some justification for starting from our own make-up, and treating as good candidates for mentality just those things whose make-up is significantly like our own. It is to this, then, that we will be addressing ourselves in the next chapter.

9: the computer and the brain

To take stock of what has arisen from the foregoing, we may sum up as follows. The most attractive approach to the mind-body problem is one which does not force us to choose between mind and matter as two rival alternatives, but which allows us to recognize the different kind of reality of each, and give it its proper place. If we are not to end up as dualists, stuck with two different types of substance and a problem about how they can interact, we must accept that the mind and the body are not two things glued trogether, as it were, but two aspects of one thing, that the answer to the question 'What is it like to be that thing?' will depend on how the thing comes by its experiences. And the question 'Is there anything it is like to be that thing at all?' is only going to be answerable by comparing its channels of experience with those of creatures which we know to be capable of conscious thought – ourselves. Now one thing forces itself on our attention: there are some kinds of things which tend to exhibit the criteria for having a mental aspect as well as a physical aspect, and some which do not. Among those which *do* are human beings, and at least those species which are towards the top end of the phylogenetic tree. Among those which *don't* are tables and chairs, rocks, vegetables, and machines such as bicycles and lawnmowers. The next question is bound to be, where do the more 'intelligent' sorts of *computers* fit into this pattern in the light of this present position?

In order to bring us closer to answering this, we will next compare briefly the overall structure, function and composition of the typical computer, with that of the human central nervous system, asking what similarities and differences might reasonably be regarded as relevant to our question. We begin with a rough sketch of the working of a computer system.

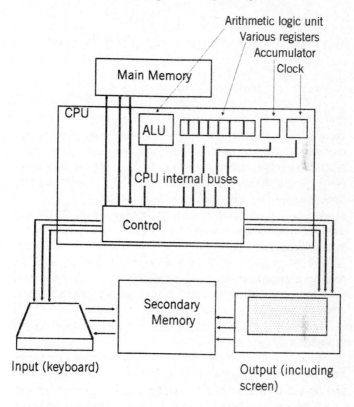

Figure 5: The main components of a conventional computer system

the mechanics of the computer

In one sense, there is no such thing as a 'typical computer', since computers come in lots of kinds, intended for different purposes and incorporating different patterns of construction (or 'architectures' as a computer scientist will say). However, it is possible to identify certain principles which are common to most machines, and certain fundamental components which any computer will contain in some shape or other. The five essential components of a computer (see figure 5) may be seen as:

(1) The central processing unit (CPU)
(2) The memory
(3) The input device(s)
(4) The output device(s)
(5) The communication path(s), or bus(es).

The CPU is the most important part of the computer and, in many modern machines, is contained on a single 'chip' (a small piece of silicon with an integrated circuit etched on to its surface). It controls and co-ordinates the operations taking place in all other parts of the system. The chief components of the CPU are: *the arithmetic-logic unit* (ALU) which actually performs the basic operations such as addition, subtraction, multiplication etc.; the *accumulator(s)*, which hold the number(s) currently in use by the ALU; the *clock*, which synchronizes those activities of the computer which need to be carried out 'in step' with each other by emitting a regular pulse; and the *registers*, which commonly include:

a *memory address register*, which holds the next memory address needed

a *memory data register*, which holds a piece of data recently brought from the memory

some *status registers*, which hold information regarding the present state of the system (e.g. whether or not we have to carry one from the last column of an addition)

some *general purpose registers*, which hold numbers needed soon or frequently by the CPU (since holding them in the main memory wastes time fetching them on each occasion)

a *program counter*, which keeps track of which instruction in a program is to be executed next

an *instruction register*, which holds the instruction currently being executed, and

a *stack pointer*, which indicates where the last item stored in the *stack* (a last-in-first-out storage space used by the CPU) is to be found.

The memory of a computer is obviously an important feature, since this is where most of the information is stored. Memory is divided into two kinds, *main memory*, and *secondary storage*. Main memory usually takes the form of a large number of 'cells' arranged in rows and columns. These cells normally consist, physically, of tiny electronic circuits on silicon, and each cell is capable only of holding one of two values (i.e. each can only hold a yes/no piece of information). The secondary storage is also contained in lots of yes/no units, but instead of being in the form of circuits constituting cells, it is usually retained by the magnetization of disks (hard or floppy), tapes, or cylinders, which can be loaded and unloaded from the computer, and stored quite separately when not required. Main memory may be lost when the machine is switched off, whereas secondary memory, of course, is not.

There are two other distinctions which ought to be made between types of memory. Firstly, *read-only memory* (ROM) is memory whose contents are a permanent part of the system, and cannot be altered by the user of the computer, wheras *read-and-write memory* (RAM) contains whatever has been put there by the user; main memory is partly ROM and partly RAM, whilst secondary storage is entirely RAM. Secondly, *random access* memory is memory which we can dive into at any chosen point (like putting a gramaphone stylus directly on to the track we require), wheras in *sequential access* memory we have to start at the beginning and work through until we come to the part we want (like trying to find a particular point on a cassette tape); main memory, disks and cylinders are random access, whilst magnetic tapes, of course, are sequential. The yes/no units of memory are known as *bits* (short for 'binary digits'). A group of eight bits is normally known as a 'byte'. Bits are also grouped into *words*, which vary in length depending on the machine in question, a common length being 16 bits (i.e. 2 bytes). A word is then the basic unit of information for that machine. Each word in the memory has a numerical *address*, that is a label for the particular location where it is to be found, identified by the rows and columns in which the memory is organized.

Input devices can be of various kinds. The most common is probably the keyboard, which receives messages typed in by the user by pressing keys corresponding to the characters of the alphabet, numbers, etc. Other sorts include, notably, those which bring information to the computer from some other device, such as a measuring instrument.

Output devices can be classified in a similar way. The most common sorts are the cathode-ray tube screen which is just like a television screen and is known as a VDU (visual display unit), and the printer; punched tape and cards used to be common, though they have now been largely superseded. Another kind of output is the transmission of information from the computer to control some other machine (e.g. to regulate a valve).

Here, a distinction should be made between *analogue* and *digital* representation of information. This is especially important with regard to input and output. We have already seen that a typical computer only handles yes/no questions (i.e. it only holds *binary* information), though in very large quantities. Clearly not all the possible input to the machine will be naturally of that kind. Of course, the input may consist of numbers alone, and numbers can easily be represented in binary form (by employing base 2 instead of base 10 for our arithmetic); but often it will be in other forms.

For example, suppose that the input is from a rain gauge, and that the computer is intended to turn on a sprinkler whenever the gauge falls below a given point. The information which forms the input does not naturally lend itself to being expressed as a series of discreet numbers, since it is a *quantity* which is constantly fluctuating: it invites not the question 'how many', but the question 'how much?' There are two ways in which a machine can handle this. On the one hand, it can incorporate some way of representing the information in a form analogous to that in which it naturally comes; this is, for obvious reasons, called *analogue* form, and a computer which employs such a method is known as an analogue computer. On the other hand, it can transform the information into digital form, by turning it into a series of discreet numbers (the readings being taken at intervals as close together as we wish); a machine employing this method is called a digital computer, and this is by far the most common sort. Clearly, the same considerations will apply, the other way round, in the case of output as in that of input. This distinction between analogue and digital methods of operation is crucial, and we shall be returning to it later.

To press on, *the buses* in a computer are the means by which one section or component of the machine is able to communicate with another. A bus consists of a number of lines along which messages can be sent, and buses tend to divide into: data bus (which carries the actual information we are dealing with at a given time), address bus (which carries information concerning where, in the memory, data is coming from or going to), and control bus (which handles information about what the system itself is currently supposed to be doing). The CPU will also probably have its own internal bus system.

Lastly, a computer will not run without *software* – the programs which tell the computer what tasks it is supposed to be performing. Apart from those programs which simply make the machine execute the specific task required by the user, two other pieces of software should be mentioned. One is the operating system, which oversees the total operation of the computer, enabling it to respond to users' programs, and doing 'behind the scenes' work such as memory management. The other is the compiler, which translates between the language the computer understands (consisting of the simple yes/no units) and the programming language used by the person who writes the programs; thus it allows us to 'talk to' the computer in a language tolerably similar to our own.

how the computer operates
In order to be clear about what is going on in the computer when it is in use, let us try to trace a single operation right through the system, taking as our example the operation of adding one number to another. It must be borne in mind that this is not a description of what happens in any given machine, but in some hypothetical machine which may be taken as typical. Suppose, then, that the instruction which the machine is to execute forms part of a program which has been loaded

into the main memory, and let us take it from there:

(i) The program counter will hold the address of the next instruction, and send it to the memory address register.

(ii) A signal is sent to the memory telling it to read from the memory address register.

(iii) Suppose that the address which the program counter sent to the memory address register was address 200; the memory now sends the word in address 200 to the memory data register.

(iv) The memory data register now holds the instruction to be executed; for the purpose of the example, suppose that the instruction (held, of course, in the form of a binary number) decodes as 'add the contents of location 750 to the result of the last operation' and places the result in address 990.

(v) The result of the last operation will be in the accumulator, since that is where all results appear; suppose it is the number 3.

(vi) The number 750 is sent to the memory address register.

(vii) A signal is sent to the memory telling it to read from memory address register.

(viii) The word in address 750 is sent to the memory data register.

(ix) Suppose that the word in 750 consists of the number 7; this number is sent to the arithmetic logic unit, which adds it to the 3 in the accumulator.

(x) Finally, the number 10, the result of the operation, is sent to memory location 990.

Notice that, though the memory has to hold two kinds of things – instructions and data – there is no *intrinsic* difference between them as they are stored. In other words, we can't tell simply by looking at a word in memory, what it is supposed to represent: the stored word 103478, for example, might mean 'add the contents of address 34 to the contents of 78', or it might just stand for the number one hundred and three thousand four hundred and seventy-eight. Which it actually means will be determined only by the context, which means by what has come before it in the program.

One reason why it has been thought desirable to go into a

little detail regarding the workings of computers, is that many people have a tendency to want to attribute 'real thought' to machines partly for the reason that they find something mysterious about how they work – just as there is something as yet mysterious about the way our own brains work. This temptation should be resisted. The first computers used cogs, gears and cards; and it is only for reasons of practicality that we cannot still build our immensely larger and more sophisticated systems in the same way. Few people would want to attribute genuine thought to a load of ironmongery; and yet electronic devices, being so small scale and their workings therefore hidden, have an unwarranted fascination for those who are quick to draw grandiose conclusions from every new development in the art.

from computers to artificial intelligence

What we have been looking at so far is computers, and a little of what it takes to make them run, the 'systems software'. But no computer considered by itself could possibly be said to be doing any thinking, even in a metaphorical sense. What makes the difference between mere computers and artificial intelligence is what we *do* with them. It is not the computer, but the whole *system*, including the programs which tell it what to do, which we call intelligent, or apparently intelligent. In this section we will look a little at some of the things people are doing, and have been doing, with computers, which constitute the discipline of artificial intelligence. First of all, however, we will have a brief glance at some of the tools of the trade for a worker in artificial intelligence.

Intelligent systems rely very heavily on *knowledge*. Leaving aside the question of whether we should put inverted commas round that word, we may divide up what the system needs in this respect into two parts: items of knowledge, and knowledge structures. The items are the individual things which the system is said to know something *about*. The designer of the system must therefore decide what kinds of things the system will be dealing with. Examples would be objects, properties of objects, relations between objects, numbers, geometrical figures, and so on. In some systems the concept of meta-knowledge is used.

Meta-knowledge is knowledge about what is known by the system itself (for example, being aware of just how much you know and how much you don't is a case of meta-knowledge).

But we also want to know how to put this knowledge together, and this is where knowledge structures come in. Probably the best-known form of knowledge structure is the state space. A state space is an arrangement of facts which allows the system to know where it can and can't go immediately from the state which it is currently considering. For example, the states might be arrangements of pieces on a chess board, and the state space would then be the arrangement of facts linking the different arrangements and telling the system which states can be brought about from which others. There are other forms of knowledge structure besides the state space. One is procedural representation, which allows the system to find its way around by an hierarchical arrangement of 'procedures', i.e. small chunks of a program. Another is production systems, which use a series of productions, which are rules, saying that *if* something is the case *then* such-and-such is to be done. A third is frames, which are, metaphorically, rather like arrangements of little pigeon holes.

Now the fact that artificial intelligence (AI as we shall henceforth call it, according to custom) relies heavily upon the idea of knowledge, has another consequence. Here we must make a distinction between two kinds of programming languages. Just as in English we have declarative sentences (or 'indicatives') such as 'The door is closed', and also imperative sentences like 'Close the door!', so there are two kinds of computer languages. One sort uses declaratives, telling the computer that something or other is the case, and the other sort uses imperatives, telling it to do something. The languages using imperatives are the older, and are referred to by the programmers and computer scientists as 'procedural languages' as opposed to 'declarative languages'. Declarative languages have, for obvious reasons, become increasingly important in AI. The two best known of these are PROLOG (whose name is meant to suggest that it is used for what is known as logic programming), and LISP (which is also supposed to bring to mind the function of the language – list processing). We now move on to glance at some of the areas which make up AI, attempting both to get a panoramic (if distant) view of the landscape, and also to try and understand what kinds of claims are being made for it. We will take these areas of interest in order.

natural language

It has long been an aim of workers in AI to produce systems capable of learning, understanding and using natural languages such as English, French or Dutch. In order to learn a language, we need to learn implicitly or explicitly how to parse an expression in it; that is, how to recognize grammatical forms and construct them for ourselves. On a computer, this is done by a program called (not unreasonably) a parser. Parsers come in two kinds: top-down and bottom-up. A top-down parser starts by considering the rules for the 'goal symbol' (the symbol we are trying to recognize, i.e. a properly constructed sentence) and goes through the different ways in which it could be constituted, until it finds one which matches the data it is given. A bottom-up parser conversely starts from the symbols it is given as data, and tries to find legitimate ways of combining them into larger units, and finally into a complete sentence.

The syntax of natural languages is, however, notoriously hard – much more complex that that of artificial languages – and contains many ambiguities. When it comes to writing a program which will not only understand but generate English sentences, we face two difficulties. One is that it will need an enormously large data base of facts, many of them just very ordinary, trivial facts about the world, in order to stand any chance of being able to take part in a dialogue with a human language-speaker. We tend to forget the sheer quantity of information which each of us carries around and which allows us to communicate with each other. The second difficulty is that of making the program sensitive to conversational situations, which are of course social situations. How we understand what is meant by something which is said to us depends greatly on the context in which it is said. It was the failure to face both of these difficulties which led to the comical results generated by ELIZA, which we saw in chapter 5. An extension of language recognition is machine-translation, and many of the problems which have to be dealt with are similar.

expert systems

Expert systems are vast systems which hold a store of knowledge in a data base, and which can be consulted by users wanting a decision based on the vast amount of data such systems can hold, and exploiting their ability to access it and process it very quickly. An example would be a medical expert system designed so as to hold a store of information about symptoms and diseases, so that a doctor could enter a patient's symptoms and get a very fast opinion on what the patient might be suffering from. The information is, of course, initially entered by doctors who have learned it from experience or from other doctors, and new information may be entered. Thus the system is said to have two modes: consultation mode (when it is giving an opinion or a decision or a piece of information) and knowledge acquisition mode (when it is 'learning' something). A further aspect of expert systems is that their constructors have often designed them in such a way that the system can explain *how* it arrived at a particular answer – which might sometimes tell us as much as the answer itself. Besides being used for actual consultation, expert systems can also be employed as an efficient way of teaching a subject, for the novice can use it as a kind of encyclopaedia. The discipline of constructing expert systems is sometimes known as 'knowledge engineering', and employs many of the tools which will be discussed in a moment when talking about problem solving.

problem solving

Many aspects of AI involve problem solving techniques, and the subject is fruitfully studied in its own right. It includes such topics as problem reduction, searching, and deduction; all of which are aspects of the way in which an intelligent system goes about solving a problem. Problem reduction means breaking down the problem into smaller 'sub-problems', then breaking these down further, and so on until it sees how a solution is possible. Searching is an important topic in computing generally. It oftens happens that a program has to search a given collection of data in order to find the one which fits a particular requirement. For example, a chess playing program would have to search through a number of possible moves to find the one which would have the desired results and none of the undesirable ones. The total structure of possibilities is called the 'search space'. Deduction is, of course, reasoning; and in order for the system to be able to draw conclusions from the premises which it has, it must have at least the elementary rules of logic built into it. Just as we found there were two directions in which a sentence parser could reason, there are also two directions in which a problem solving program can reason. It can use *forward reasoning*, which begins with the given situation and tries at each stage to bring it nearer to fulfilling the goal condition, or *backward reasoning*, which starts from the goal condition and breaks it down into sub-goals, then breaks those down, and so on until all the final sub-goals are fulfilled by the given situation. Thus a bottom-up parser might be said to reason forwards, and a top-down parser to reason backwards.

Among the specialized areas within problem solving are theorem proving, which is of particular interest to logicians, mathematicians and, of course, computing scientists, and game playing. Computers can be programmed to play many games very well, even games as complex as chess, which was mentioned above (though there is no existing chess-playing program which cannot be beaten by a master). There even exist chess-playing programs which are capable of improving their own performance by learning from experience.

vision and pattern recognition
For some purposes it is necessary to have machines which can 'see', and which can recognize certain patterns in what they 'see' so that they can reidentify situations and behave accordingly. Seeing, in human beings, involves not just passively

receiving stimuli through the eyes, but also a great deal of interpretation, most of which is done subconsciously. It is to be expected, then, that building a system which is capable of 'seeing' and making sense of what it 'sees', will be a complex task. It must be programmed to recognize certain configurations of lines and corners, in such a way as to allow it to pick out geometrical shapes. It must also be made to have some grasp of perspective – to interpret the input data as three dimensional objects, and to identify their relative spatial positions, which object is behind or in front of another, and so on. This is an aspect of 'pattern recognition', though there is more to pattern recognition than the identification of visual patterns – natural language programs, for example, may be said to employ pattern recognition in looking for certain configurations of words in the input data. Some aspects of visual pattern recognition are extremely difficult to program into a machine. The recognition of people's faces, for instance, which is very important in human life, and which we are quite good at, is almost impossible for an artificial device. One reason for this, is that we know very little as yet about how we ourselves do it. The importance of having real (as opposed to merely symbolic) input from the world, and being able to make sense of it, will be seen in the next chapter to be of great philosophical importance.

voice recognition

Another aspect of it is voice recognition, which of course is one aspect – the most important aspect – of the interpretation of incoming sound. Its significance for the future of interaction between human beings and intelligent machines is obvious. Research in this field began by devising systems capable of recognizing single words when spoken to them through a microphone. The next step was to get them to identify correctly connected sequences of words, which is especially difficult due to the way in which words run into one another in the spoken language, and the sounds of words alter depending on those of the surrounding words. Other difficulties are that the sounds which we give to words vary depending on individual speakers, on regional dialects, and on the social context and emotions of the speaker (whether said with surprise, delight, disbelief etc.). Some success has been achieved in this field, with systems having a vocabulary of around a thousand words. (Compare this, however, with the enormous vocabulary of a language such as Japanese.)

robotic control
Another aspect of interaction with the world, apart from the interpretation of incoming data, is the ability to manipulate the world – here the causal interaction is in the opposite direction. Robots are, of course, already extensively used in industry, in the manufacture of cars for example. These robots are very far from the quasi-human robots of science fiction. Most actual robots consist only of a single arm: the task of making such an artificial arm function intelligently is sufficiently difficult in itself. Amongst other things, it requires some of the techniques of 'problem solving' discussed above. The 'state space' for the robot will be a set of facts about its physical surroundings, known as a 'world model'. This will be given in terms of a co-ordinate geometry. What is also required is some equivalent of the kinesthetic sense in human beings: this is the sense which tells you where the parts of your body are, but 'from the inside', as it were, so that you know what position your own arm is in even with your eyes shut. The robot will, then, be rather in the position of a person with closed eyes, being told 'go left one unit, down two units, right one unit' and so on. Unless, of course, we combine machine vision with robotic control, so that the system discovers for itself where things are, and can then obey instructions about what to do with them.

learning
We saw above that there already exist, for example, some chess-playing programs which are capable of learning from experience and thereby improving their play over a certain number of games, as a human player does. This idea of building a learning faculty into an artificial system clearly has a large bearing on the enterprise of attempting to stimulate real human intelligence. We have already seen some successes in 'auto-

matic programs' i.e. programs which write programs, and some headway is being made with programs which are self-modifying – which can re-write themselves.

personal qualities

Many people feel that, even with all this intelligence, or 'intelligence', there is something about human beings which the artificial system fails to capture. Some work has been done on attempting to program personal qualities into a system – especially, of course, in natural-language-using systems which interact with human beings. Opinions vary concerning the success of existing attempts and the prospect for future ones in this direction. It is perhaps significant that the most convincing results have been achieved where the simulated personality was intended to be in a neurotic or psychotic condition characterized by a limited repertoire of behaviour.

Before considering the bearing of all this on the issues with which we are concerned, let us move on to the second topic of this chapter, which is meant to invite comparision with the above. This is an excursion into the physiology of the central nervous system.

the mechanics of human thought

What follows is an even rougher outline of the organization of the physical apparatus of thought in human beings, than that which was given above of the organization of the computer. It is intended merely as an indication of the basic structures and their functions, and not as a *vade mecum* of brain surgery! It must also be borne in mind that the workings of the human brain are far less well understood than those of the most sophisticated computer. With a computer, we work from man-made blueprints to the finished machine: with the brain, we start from the complete article and try, as it were, to reconstruct the blueprints.

The section of the human anatomy which is uniquely associated with thinking is the *central nervous system*, the chief components of which are the brain and the spinal cord (the chief pathway through the nervous system). Of these, the brain is by far the more important to us here. The building blocks of which organisms are made up are, of course, *cells*. In the nervous system, these take the form of *nerve cells*, or *neurones*, as they are usually called. Neurones have the special feature of being subject to a kind of electro-chemical event known as *arousal* of a neurone. When aroused, the neurone 'fires', i.e. discharges an electrical impulse. This impulse can cause the arousal of nearby neurones, thus being capable of setting up a chain reaction. The gaps between neurones are known as *synapses*, and the arousal of one neurone by another obviously takes place across the synapse.

The opposite of a state of arousal is a state of *inhibition*. If a region of the nervous system is inhibited, this means that the arousal of nerve cells is inhibited by a special mechanism: for example, if you thrust your hand close up to a hot fire, your nervous system will automatically inhibit the nerves tending to move the hand in the direction of the heat, so that your hand in involuntarily withdrawn.

This brings us to the distinction between the *autonomic nervous system*, and the part which is concerned with conscious thought. This distinction is of obvious significance for our purposes. The autonomic system deals with those functions of the body which do not involve conscious thought, such as breathing and the circulation of the blood (things we can do in our sleep). The non-autonomic part of the nervous system handles those functions which are subject to conscious control. It is not, however, easy to separate the physical areas of the brain into autonomous and non-autonomous categories.

When we begin to look at the division of structure and function within the brain, we find that it too falls naturally into five parts (see figure 6). These are:

(1) The cerebral hemispheres

(2) The interbrain, consisting chiefly of the thalamus and hypothalamus

(3) The midbrain

(4) The afterbrain, comprising the pons and the cerebellum

(5) The medulla oblongata.

Leaving what is probably the most important until last, we may very roughly sketch the main respective functions of these regions as follows.

The thalamus serves to integrate incoming nerve impulses from the sense organs, and relays them to the cerebral cortex (which we shall look at in a moment).

The hypothalamus deals largely with drives and their satiation (arousing and inhibiting as appropriate) including eating, drinking, sleeping and reproduction (by means of sex hormones), besides some aspects of emotional expression; it also controls the pituitary gland (the most important of the glands, which secretes hormones into the blood), and controls the balance of water in the body.

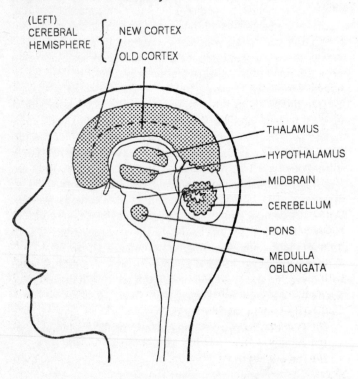

Figure 6 Structure of the human brain

The midbrain handles some simple reflexes concerned with seeing and hearing (for example the movement of the pupils of the eyes).

The pons contains the points of origin of some of the *motor nerves*, which are the nerves taking information from the brain to other parts of the body to initiate action (e.g. the motor nerves controlling bodily movement and posture originate in the pons); it also contains the terminations (i.e. the 'other ends') of some of the sensory nerves (which are the ones going in the opposite direction, taking information from the body to the brain), especially those to do with the sense of touch, with pain, with bodily temperature, and with hearing and the position of the head.

The cerebellum deals with the co-ordination of posture and locomotion (walking, running, etc.).

The medulla oblongata is really an extension of the spinal cord; it contains and integrates both sensory and motor pathways (of which there are many in the nervous system, all with specialized functions) and also handles the automatic functions of blood circulation and respiration.

The cerebral hemispheres are complex structures, dealing largely with perception and the interpretation of incoming sensory information, and with learning and memory. A hemisphere may be divided into two regions, each of which is known as a cortex. The *old cortex* is the simpler, and is found in many animals other than man. It regulates certain aspects of the body, and of the emotions, and includes a 'motor area', a 'sensory area', and an 'association area' which deals with associating and co-ordinating ideas to form coherent mental patterns. The *new cortex* only appears in this form in man, and is evolutionarily more recent, as its name suggests. It contains a number of 'lobes', notably:

the occipital lobes which are concerned with sight

the temporal lobes dealing with hearing and language

the parietal lobes which integrate sensory information from skin and muscles, and

the frontal lobes which are to do with movement and posture.

The new cortex also handles some associative functions more sophisticated than those in the association area of the old cortex, and which are still very imperfectly understood. Furthermore, the new cortex *in the left hemisphere only* contains a *speech centre*. The cerebral hemispheres, then, form the area of the brain most associated with the activities which we think of as being intelligent and voluntary, and also with personality, disposition, temperament, and ethical thinking. It should also be noted, in passing, that the main connections between the left cerebral hemisphere and the rest of the body, are with the *right* side of the body, whilst the right hemisphere connects principally with the *left* side.

What we cannot do here, as we did in the case of the computer, is to trace a particular operation right through the system, and show in detail what is involved. We cannot do this, not simply from lack of space, but because it cannot be done: as was pointed out at the start of this section, we are only just in the process of 'reconstructing the blueprints' of the central nervous system. Prompted by this consideration, then, we will go on to ask what seem to be the major overall similarities and differences in principle between human thought mechanism and the working of a computer or intelligent system. This, it is to be hoped, will shed some light on the question of how far the physical make-up of (some) machines invites us to attribute a mental as well as a physical aspect to them.

some similarities
The most obvious, and seemingly trivial, similarity between machines and the human brain, is that they are both physical objects. Despite the apparent triviality of this observation, there is a point to it. For if we accept, as we have, that the seat of thought in a human being is the brain, then the answer to the question 'Is it possible to have a physical system which really thinks?' is already answered in the affirmative. And oddly enough, it is this question which has been a major source of contention between writers in the past. However, it is of course open to those who answer this question in the negative, to expand upon it by saying something like 'a *purely* physical

system'. Thus, whilst admitting that the brain plays an important role in human thought, the anti-materialist may still wish to insist that real conscious thought is nevertheless impossible without some shadowy non-physical ingredient. And naturally, a person who wishes to insist on this will be very hard to answer, for reasons similar to those for which the solipsist was difficult to answer: direct evidence either for or against his position is impossible to come by (unless, of course, by 'non-physical ingredient' he happens to mean merely something like structures, patterns, rules or principles, in which case the argument will be of a rather different sort).

Further, it is clear that human brains and computers do some of the same jobs, though the extent to which even this is true is often exaggerated. For example, the exponents of artificial intelligence sometimes talk as though the creation of a computer system which matched the intelligence of a human being would be equivalent to simulating human intelligence, forgetting that human beings have many other qualities other than intelligence. Conversely, some of the things which machines are very good at (such as doing huge 'brute force' searches through masses of data) are things at which human beings are quite poor. This is perhaps a good point at which to emphasise the fact that we must beware of the idea of artificial intelligence as merely the mimicking of human intelligence, as though the whole purpose of designing intelligent machines were to create electronic replicas of ourselves.

But what most concerns us at this point, is the existence of some alleged similarities between the structure and operation of the two physical systems, i.e. the human brain and certain sorts of modern computer. One reason why this is important, is that if it can be shown that there are significant similarities of structure and function between them, this will strengthen the case of those who argue that genuine thought in machines is possible, and weaken the position of the sceptic who points out the lack of criteria for deciding how likely it is that this might be the case.

Firstly, it is easy for it to appear, on the surface, that both the brain and the computer use *language*. It seems, as we noted in chapter 4, that is is language which enables human beings to have the capacity for concept-formation, and hence for thought, that they have. It further appears to be the case that we have an inbuilt capacity for learning and using language, and to respond to verbal stimuli. And is it not also the case that the computer represents things to itself linguistically?

Unfortunately, this is not really true. For the 'verbal' abilities of computers are largely illusory. For a computer to 'recognise' a word, for example, it must go through the list of all the words it 'knows', and check the present one letter-for-letter against each. Compare this with the instantaneous recognition of a familiar word, of which people are capable. In the case of recognising faces, the difference is even more striking. Of course, it is possible that the same sort of thing is going on as in a computer whenever we recognise a word or a face, except unconsciously and very quickly. However, even this seems not to be quite right. We will have more to say about representation in a moment.

Secondly, and more importantly, it is often remarked that both the brain and the average computer, ancient or modern, work on the binary principle. That is, they are both composed of elements which have two states – 'on' and 'off'. In the case of the brain, these elements are the neurones, whilst in the case of the machine they are sometimes like electronic switches. All the 'higher level' operations of both, so the story goes, are built up in much the same way from essentially the same sort of ultimate components.

The trouble with this supposed parallel is partly that it seems not to be strictly true, since the neurones of the brain have been shown to operate partly on a binary digital principle, but also partly on an analogue (continuous rather than two-state) basis. It may be that the binary ingredient is the important one with regard to the way in which thought processes are brought about, and that the analogue element is subsidiary to this function. But moreover, the firing or non-firing of neurones in the brain does not really correspond to the opening and closing of switches, or 'gates' in a computer's circuits: the brain does not appear to use these binary operations in a way analogous to the way they are used in a switching network, as logical operations, but merely as ways of opening or closing various communication channels. Or at least, it has never been shown that there is a more significant resemblance in this respect.

However that may be, it does not affect the next point, which is that even if it were shown that this parellel holds, it would still be unclear what would follow from it. For, although we would be assured that, at bottom level, something like the same components were being used, the analogy would still be so general as to leave things hopelessly vague. Many things work on a binary principle besides brains and digital computers, and to argue the possibility of conscious thought in machines direectly from their binary nature would be a bit like arguing that a sufficiently sophisticated radio could be made to do the job of a spaceship, since both have transistors in them!

some differences

If the supposed similarities between the operation of a computer and that of the human brain seem much thinner than is sometimes supposed, the most obvious differences are comparatively profound. Perhaps the most significant of these (and maybe even so glaring that it is often overlooked) is the organic nature of the brain, contrasted to the inorganic, mechanistic character of a computer or computing system. Human nervous systems grow, whereas machines are built. Another, closely related, difference, lies in the material out of which brains and machines respectively are built: machines being composed of 'hardware' whereas our nervous systems are composed of what someone has christened 'wetware' i.e. organic tissue.

Yet the trouble with picking these things out as significant differences is rather like that of highlighting the supposed similarity of being based on the binary principle, which was discussed above. For it is seriously unclear what conclusions, if any, can be drawn from such a fact. The idea that this difference can be used to drive a wedge between the 'real' thought of human beings and the merely artificial 'thought' of machines, seems once again to be based on nothing stronger than the assumption that things are good candidates for genuine thought only insofar as they resemble us in certain ways. The problem here clearly lies in the question: *Which* ways, *which* resemblances are important?

Two things are worth mentioning here. Firstly, the structure of a thing would seem more important in this respect than the material out of which it is made. There seems to be no good reason why carbon-based creatures as such should have the capacity for thought whilst similarily structured creatures composed of other substances should not. Secondly, however, there is an important qualitative difference between organic and non-organic things, which lies in the capacity of the organic to interact with its environment in ways in which the inorganic cannot. This has been touched on already, and will be discussed in more detail in chapter 10.

One other result of the inorganic nature of machines, is that their parts can be swapped about in a way in which the parts of people cannot. Leaving aside such tricky issues as that of the implications of brain transplants, we may point to a feature such as the peripheral memory which computers have. Is there anything connected with human beings to compare with this? Can such things as books, libraries and tape recordings be regarded as human peripheral memory? The answer seems to be: not in quite the same sense. All of these latter are just part of the external world for a human being, whereas they are actually 'loaded into' a machine. The computer makes no distinction between those bits of software which are 'part of' itself and what is merely perceived or read from without. Even a machine's operating system which we can, perhaps, think of as the equivalent of a human being's personality, may be stored peripherally, and only loaded when required.

Another, and slightly more technical way in which the human brain has sometimes been identified as unlike a computing system, is to do with the fact that they seem to represent the objects of their thought in radically different ways. As we have seen, a computer is apt to hold a given piece of data in a particular location. Thus on the whole it is true to say that if we ask 'Where in this machine is the representation of Mr. Jones, or of Paris, or the Financial Times Index, held?', there will be some determinate answer to the question, in terms of particular chunks of the machine's memory. It seems characteristic of the brain, on the other hand, that representations are not localised, but 'distributed'. That is to say, we could surgically remove any given portion of the brain without necessarily destroying any individual representation – and not because there is a duplicate, but because that representation did not reside in any one specific location in the first place. This has sometimes been explained by reference to the example of the 'Grandmother Neurone': if representations in the brain were localised as in most computers, then there ought to be some cell, or maybe cluster of cells, which correspond to the concept 'Grandmother', such that, if we removed that cell or cluster of cells, the patient would be unable to think about his, or any other, grandmother! All his other concepts would remain in place, but that specific one would be lost, until he reacquired it by learning. This, however, is not the case – indeed, it is barely conceivable – which gives rise to the supposition that representation in the brain works on a different principle from representation in the kind of computer described above – the usual kind, in this respect.

Partly in response to this challenge, some recent workers in Artificial Intelligence have developed a kind of system whose operation with regard to representation (and therefore, importantly, to learning also) is claimed to resemble that of the human brain much more closely that any hitherto constructed, and to embody a qualitative difference of principle from that of the traditional computer. This departure is worth a special mention here, and we will conclude this chapter with a brief look at it.

machines that mimic the mind?

The kind of machines, or rather of machine 'architecture', which are currently in vogue tend to go under the generic heading of 'connectionist'. Thus connectionism, as it is known, has a claim to a special place in present-day thinking about the design of machines intended for use in the field of Artificial Intelligence. As suggested above, these architectures differ from traditional approaches to computer organization in the way they approach the representation of the objects with which they are supposed to deal. Representation in connectionist architectures is meant to be 'distributed' (as it appears to be in the human brain) rather than 'localized' (as in the traditional computer structure).

What makes this possible, according to the exponents of this kind of design, is that, instead of having a single central processing unit (CPU), or a few similar processors, the connectionist machine contains a large number (potentially many thousands) of processors, which are correspondingly far simpler than those of the more conventional machine. The idea is that these 'processing units' should operate in parallel, each performing a very trivial message-passing function. The crux of the strategy is that, rather than an object being represented within some one element, or group of elements in the machine, the representation resides in the *connections* between the elements. These connections may have varying strengths, making it possible to build up a potentially enormous number of possible configurations. Once we see the representation of the object, or concept ('grandmother' or whatever) as being retained in the pattern of connections and connection strengths, we can understand how this differs from the conventional computer architecture, and at the same time how it can be claimed that such structures reproduce the way in which concepts are grasped and retained in the brain more faithfully than in any other kind of device hitherto developed.

It will also be fairly clear why proponents of the connectionist argument claim that machines constructed on these principles are actually able to *learn*, rather than merely spoon-fed with data. For concepts can be implanted gradually, an element at a time, each augmentation of a connection-strength rendering it easier for representations to be further built up along the pathways already established. As is apparently the case with human beings, the acquisition of concepts, or of associations between them, need not be an 'all-or-nothing', 'on-or-off' affair, but rather a matter of gradual building, strengthening, and, of course, adjustment where necessary. In other words, a process of genuine learning.

It seems, then, that whilst we have discovered the conventional computer and the human brain to be very widely different in their structure and functioning, there are signs that research may be moving in the direction of *rapprochement*. Whilst it is fairly clear that no currently extant machines look like good candidates for doing the same jobs (much less in the same *way*) as human nervous systems, there appears to be no reason in principle why machines should not be constructed which perform the same kinds of tasks by analogous means. Of this, more in chapter 11. For the present, however, we will pursue our discussion in the light of what has already been said, bearing in mind especially the considerations which were raised in chapter 5 regarding the significance of communication as a guide to what might or might not be 'really thinking'.

10: some further arguments

The last point is probably the most important of all. As we saw earlier in the book, the kinds of machines to which people are often tempted to ascribe conscious thought are commonly ones with no human-like qualities at all. We have noticed in the last chapter, however, that some machines in the area known as artificial intelligence do behave in a number of human-like ways. Now in chapter 5 we asked the question 'How could we get a computer to use genuine (as opposed to merely 'canned') language?', though no answer was given to this question. It is time to draw some of these threads together.

the importance of sentience

Might it be that the ability to do what some 'artificially intelligent' machines do, to play an active role in the world, to interact with and manipulate one's environment, plays a critical role in our ability to use language in the full sense? Most modern thinkers would certainly say this is so. The argument for it is, roughly, that it is in this kind of interaction and manipulation that we learn to apply the concepts which, taken together, make us into language-users. Here, we can also see what is wrong with the temptation to attribute real thought to a machine which does no more than sit on a desktop: there is no way (linguistic or otherwise) in which it could have *learned* the concepts which would have to be the tools of its thought. But having recognized that a static, inanimate machine has no way of acquiring concepts, we must not therefore assume that the only prerequisite for thought is animation, even if by that we understand systematic movement, manipulation and so on. What will also be required is some form of perception, in other words *sentience*.

The reason for wanting to say this, is that if machines are to be supposed to think, there has to be something which they think *about*. Here, it is perhaps appropriate to take a slight detour via the concept which we met in chapter 3, of *intentionality*. We will remember that intentionality is the property of being about something, i.e. of having an *object*. It occurs in language, for sentences, speeches and books can be about something; and the reason why it can occur in language is that it occurs in the mind – our thoughts are thoughts about something. Now the philosophers who make use of the concept of intentionality tend to be divided over the question of whether all of what is mental is intentional or not, that is, whether there can be non-intentional mental states. Those who believe there can, point to such mental states as being in pain, which appears to have no object, whilst those who hold that the intentional is co-extensive with the mental argue that being in pain can be regarded as a state of mind of which the pain is the intentional object. Now although we have hitherto accepted mere sensations as being sufficient for mentality (for there being something it is like to be the thing in question), it is important to recognize that a creature which had nothing but 'raw feels' would hardly be a good candidate for being a thinking thing. And furthermore, it is thinking rather than feeling which machines are supposed to be good at. Either way, there is certainly a point to saying that true thought must be, at least sometimes, *about* something.

From this it follows that the feels and sensations, if not sufficient, are at least necessary to thought. For they form our link with the outside world, the world of things that can be thought about. If we are tempted to suppose that a non-sentient creature can nevertheless be doing some real thinking, we might like to consider the following example, the outline of which was invented by the philosopher John Searle. Imagine yourself to be alone in a small room, which you may never leave. The only communication between the room and the outside world is through a slot in the wall. You can't see out of the slot, but occasionally a card is pushed in from the outside, with some characters written on it in Chinese – and we will also assume that you do not know Chinese. But you have been taught what to *do* with the sequences of characters, in the sense that you know what response to give to a given sequence of characters. For you also have a pile of cards with Chinese characters on them inside the room, and you have been instructed which sequences to push out through the slot in response to a given sequence pushed in.

It ought to be clear that, assuming the above to be all that you know, you cannot be said to understand Chinese, or to be *saying* anything when you construct your Chinese sequence. You may, of course, be taking part in some activity, and even performing a very useful service. You might, for example, be a data base giving the name of the capital city of any given country when the name of that country is pushed through the slot. But then again, for all you know you may be giving someone the prices of drinks in a bar. The point is that in this situation you could not be said to *know* anything about the outside world at all, though the information contained on the cards may well be a source of knowledge to anyone who can decipher it.

The parallel with a simple computer should be obvious. It has symbols put into it, it manipulates the symbols, and it gives symbols as output; but nothing is going on which should lead us to suppose that the machine knows what they refer to. There is, therefore, no pressure to beieve that there is anything which the machine could be thinking *about*, unless it is the symbols themselves. And to say it is thinking about the symbols themselves gets us nowhere as regards the supposed parallel with human thinking, for it is analogous to saying that what we think about is configurations of impulses in our brains rather than things in the world around us.

The fact is that we learn the concept of redness, for example, by actually seeing red things. It may be objected that a machine could come to understand concepts by being given information (in its own code, of course) about the things to which they refer. For example, that a machine might know something about what 'red' is by being fed the information that roses are red. But this 'information' is just more of the same thing. It is true that we ourselves acquire some of our concepts by purely linguistic means (I am *told* that a black hole is a concentration of gravitational energy, and thus acquire the concept without ever having experienced one), but the way in which we get a grasp on all concepts learned in this way is ultimately via concepts which are *not* learned in this way. For the machine which is given the 'information' that roses are red, this is not actually information at all since, besides not knowing what redness is, it doesn't know what a rose is either. One cannot explain something which is obscure by linking it with something equally obscure, and in this case the machine will still end up not knowing a red rose from a hole in the ground – unless, of course, it can indeed have experiences in much the same way as we do. Otherwise, it will be just like giving the person in the Chinese room example the 'information' that Moscow is cold, by simply giving him the Chinese for 'Moscow is cold'. This is one important difference between the genuine use of language and the 'canned' variety: genuine language use 'hooks on to' the world via experience and learning.

on being an organism

From the above, we may conclude that a creature cannot be said to have thought unless it can be thinking *about* something, and that it cannot be said to be thinking about something unless there are channels through which it can acquire the relevant concepts. Now these channels must, for the same reason, involve direct access to the objects of thought, in the following sense: that the information about the objects does not come in the form of representations in some linguistic notation, but as the objects out of which linguistic concepts can be constructed. Think once again, for a moment, of the Chinese Room example. The reason why the person in the room cannot be said to possess the concepts which the Chinese symbols stand for, is that what he has are merely representations of the objects to which the concepts refer, but in a language which he has never learned – and that this stock of representations, along with the different permutations of them which he knows how to construct, exhausts the content of his world. Without direct access to at least some of the possible objects of thought, the machine's world, like that of the inhabitant of the Chinese room, is going to be devoid of any semantics (i.e. empty of meanings).

Now the possibility of direct access to objects, in the above sense, is going to be dependent on the possession of some sense organs, and of some arrangement of nerves, or the equivalent, by which information can be transmitted from the outside world to the central areas of the creature's controlling system. These need not be ears, eyes, nerves made up of electro-chemical nerve cells etc. In this case we may harmlessly adopt the functionalist strategy (see chapter 7) of saying that any things which stand in the corresponding causal roles will count as being the same kinds of things: they will qualify as being sense organs. And since we also observed that *acting on* the world is important for learning, as well as being *acted on* by the world, we will also require something corresponding to the organs by means of which we manipulate our environment; and this will also have to satisfy the criterion of directness outlined above. As far as artificial intelligence is concerned, these sensory organs and manipulatory organs take the form of sensory transducers and motor transducers – the devices which convert the external stimuli into digital electronic form, and the appropriate internal electronic impulses into physical action, respectively.

Note, by the way, that the fact that external stimuli have to be converted into digital form does not necessarily reduce the machine to the status of the occupant of the Chinese room. It is merely the form which the stimulus takes for the machine, and its role is purely causal: it is not meant as a representation of anything, in the linguistic sense, any more than the pattern of neural activity in my nerves is a linguistic representation of the stimulus which gave rise to it – I do not have to learn to interpret it as being a sensation of heat, or a blow on the head.

Of course, any amount of input and output via transducers is not going to guarantee that the creature in question is actually sentient. We have seen that, even in the case of human beings, there is not a logically doubtproof guarantee that other people are sentient. This was the point of formulating the requirement of directness above: it is meant as a necessary though probably not a sufficient criterion for sentience, which will have to serve our purposes at least for the time being, in the absence of a criterion which is both necessary and sufficient. However, what is not open to doubt about other people on the grounds of other minds scepticism, is that they are organisms. Being an organism is *par excellence* a functional property and not a mental one. Now it seems to follow from the foregoing that any artifact which is at all a candidate for possessing genuine thought, is going to be an organism. To say that something is an organism is, in fact, to say even less than that it has this directness of input and output with the world; plants, for example, are organisms, but they have no real nervous system. The proper conclusion, then, is that anything capable of actual thought is at least going to be an organism. The question which now suggests itself is whether something which is an organism can at the same time be a machine. We will not attempt to answer this question here, however, but will look first at another aspect of the background to thought in the full sense.

having thoughts and having purposes

Plants, as we noticed just now, are organisms, and yet they rate as poor candidates for thinking – even poorer than the lower animals. Why should this be, given that both are organisms but non-language-users? An obvious reason which springs to mind is that plants do not, in the normal sense, have a nervous system. There is, therefore, much less reason to believe that they actually feel anything. Another reason, however, lies in the idea introduced above, of ability to manipulate the environment. On the whole, this is something which animals do, and plants don't do. There are borderline cases, of course: amoebas are not very manipulative, but Venus fly traps are. These are not important. What is important is the fact that the ability to think – to use concepts – is not just dependent on having sensations, but also on the kind of interaction with the world which makes concept-learning a possibility. So far we have left this rather vague; it is now time to look at the reason for it in more detail.

It is now a platitude in educational circles that learning depends very much upon doing. Young children are taught by being encouraged to take part in activities, to interact with their surroundings. This principle is obviously sound. The only trouble is that many people take it to be an empirical principle; that is, something which has been discovered from experience to be true, but which might have been found not to be true. Such people talk as though being unable to manipulate the environment in any way would merely be a rather bad handicap. That this is not the case can be revealed by considering the position of a creature without the means for any such interaction – a creature which is only a passive receiver of incoming stimuli. How could the learning process ever get off the ground at all in such a creature?

To begin with, learning of any kind depends upon having mastered some concepts. The acquisition of concepts is logically prior to the acquisition of facts: one can't learn that roses are red without knowing how to recognise redness or a rose. The way we acquire most of our concepts is by learning the use of words. The response of others to our correct or incorrect applications of words teaches us when a concept is and is not applicable: it teaches us the *extension*, in other words, of the concept. There may possibly be some sense in which non-language-users can acquire concepts, but it may safely be assumed (for reasons discussed in chapter 4) to be peripheral. Now language, and the application of concepts, are *rule-governed* activities in the Wittgensteinian sense (also outlined in chapter 4). And to have mastered a rule is to have learned how to do something correctly, how to recognize appropriate applications from misapplications. From this we may deduce that any creature capable of mastering a rule-governed activity must possess a basic grasp of what it is to do something correctly; in other words, of the concept of correctness.

This might seem to some like too strong a conclusion. They might object that there is a difference between being capable of learning the distinction between the correct and incorrect application, say of a word, and possessing the concepts of correctness in general. And that only the former is necessary to make rule-governed activity possible. For example, it may be suggested that the mere fact of having been trained to respond in the right way to a given word is sufficient evidence that a rule has been grasped, without the trainee having the idea of what it is to be correct about other things, or of what it is that all cases of correctness have in common.

In response to such an objection we may ask where the motivation is supposed to come from, on the part of the trainee, to do those things which conform to the rule in question; if it is not the desire to do what is correct in the circumstances, what is it? Take the case of a rat which has been trained to jump through hoops. There are three possibilities to account for the success of the training:

(a) The rat possesses the concept of correctness, and wishes to learn the correct way to jump through hoops,

(b) The rat just likes jumping through hoops,

(c) The rat is rewarded with food whenever it performs the actions successfully, and that is what makes the training possible.

Presumably we may discount the first hypothesis in the case of rats, which is why we have used this example. And if the second is the explanation, then surely no real training is going on: I cannot be said to have trained a creature to do something which it would have done in any case. What about the last? It is true that a rat trained to perform a trick by being bribed with cheese, is nevertheless *trained*: the question is, does this add up to having learned a piece of rule-governed activity, in the required sense? And it seems that it does not.

To distinguish between mere training and rule-following, we must appeal to an important distinction, between *prescriptive rules* and *constitutive rules*. As the name suggests, a prescriptive rule prescribes something, in other words it tells us what to do. A constitutive rule, on the other hand, tells us what constitutes doing something. Thus 'keep off the grass' is a prescriptive rule – it tells us what we must do. The rules of chess, however, are not prescriptive but constitutive – they tell us what constitutes playing chess. 'The bishop can only move diagonally' does not tell us we must not move them any other way in the same sense that 'Keep off the grass' tells us we must not walk on the grass; nothing will happen to us if we do not, except that we will no longer be playing chess.

The significance of the distinction for us is this: rule-governed activity in our sense, has to do with *constitutive* rules – especially with the rules of language – and not with prescriptive rules. And rules which are only observed because they are enforced by rewards and punishments, are prescriptive rules only. What the rat is attempting to do is not to perform the hoop trick correctly, but to obtain food; and food-gathering, however sophisticated, is not a rule-governed activity in the appropriate sense. Only if some evidence were to emerge suggesting that the rat understood and took an interest in the activity as something independent from the reward, would we say that the rat knew what constituted doing the hoop trick correctly, as opposed to saying simply that it knew how to get food effectively. A creature which is really following a rule can be expected, for example, to reflect on what it is doing, especially in borderline cases, when it will be inclined to try and sharpen up its own conception of what it is that makes a correct application different from a misapplication.

Of course, a human being who has been taught to count, for example, might well have been trained initially by being bribed with sweets and suchlike. The difference between this case and the rat is that the human being will go on to understand the activity and its point irrespective of its association with the confectionary, and is likely to retain the concepts for an indefinite time after the training has ceased, which is not the case with such creatures as rats. People learn, for example, that the activity of counting is applicable in areas other than the one in which they acquired the skill, and can typically go on to expand their grasp of the activity in the absence of further training. It should now be clear why we cannot allow that the mere fact of being trainable to do a particular thing in the way which happens to be correct, adds up to an ability to be guided by rules. It has to be accepted, therefore, that what is required for the latter is at least some grasp of what it is to do something correctly in general.

Now to possess the concept of doing something correctly, what a creature must be further capable of is having purposes. To know what it is for a piece of rule-governed behaviour to be correct, is to know the distinction between achieving and failing to achieve a given goal, the goal of applying the rule in the right way. Thus any such creature must be able to engage in goal-orientated action. This is, of course, also something which tends to go along with being an organism.

We have come a long way in this section, and before moving on, it may be useful to recapitulate a little. It has been argued that genuine thinking implies the use of concepts, that the application of concepts is a rule-governed activity, that the possibility of mastering a rule-governed activity depends on possessing the concept of doing something correctly, and that the possession of this concept involves a knowledge of what it is to have purposes, or goals. In the next two sections we will look further at the idea of purposiveness, and its importance for the question of whether machines can truly think.

purpose as reflectiveness

The idea of purposiveness harks back to a topic which was raised in the first chapter – that of creativity, or originality. Remember that this was not intended to mean anything especially spiritual or artistic, but only to refer to some everyday capacities which all human beings and many animals have, such as being able to instigate interest in a particular topic or to do something for one's own reasons. This notion of reasons will emerge as important later. Another term for what we are talking about might be *self-motivation*. It tends to be typical of machines, even very sophisticated ones, that they are not self-motivated. Although we call certain kinds of machines 'automata' (because they are in a sense 'automatic'), what their behaviour is not, is autonomous. However 'clever' what they do might be, they merely do what they are programmed to do – no more and no less. What, then, is the difference between this and the way human beings behave?

Suppose someone were to argue as follows. Human beings have a particular repertoire of behaviour, in which they engage in more or less predictable ways. Every few hours they become hungry, and then they eat. At rather longer intervals they become tired and they sleep. They are also subject to the desire for relaxation, which they indulge when they are not either sleeping, or working to earn their food and relaxation. This account would, of course, need to be expanded in order to make it look anything approaching complete. But does it not seem intuitively plausible that an account of the human behavioural repertoire could, in principle, be given, which would show human behaviour as the kind of thing which might be describable by a computer-type program?

This is by no means an easy question, and threatens to embroil us in the whole problem of the freedom of the will, which we will touch on in the next section. That will be the second of two approaches to the above challenge. First, we will consider purpose in terms of that capacity which human beings have to *reflect* on their actions in an open-ended way. Reflection might be seen as a matter of taking one's deliberation 'one step higher', of examining one's own reasons from a detached point of view. An open-ended capacity for reflectiveness therefore involves being able not only to examine our own reasons, but to go on to examine the reasons which we use in assessing the first reasons, and then to examine *those* reasons, and so on without any theoretical limit. Take, for example, the following 'interior monologue':

> 'I am hungry, therefore I have good reason to eat.'
> 'But I am on a diet, therefore I should not.'
> 'However, dieting ought not to be taken to extremes.'
> 'But I promised I would keep to the diet, and the promise should be kept irrespective of the good or harm which comes of it.'
> 'Nevertheless, there are circumstances in which it is justifiable to break a promise in order to avoid harm.'
> And so on...

Notice that this monologue is not simply a case of 'On the one hand...' and 'On the other hand'. At each stage the reasons used to support the conclusion of the last stage are examined and criticised. What is important is the fact that there is no point at which the process of standing back from one's previous reason and assessing *it*, must stop. Theoretically it could go on for ever. Now this seems to be a feature which has not yet been captured by artificial intelligence, though this is not to say that it could not be. The trouble is that a lot of obscurity surrounds the question of what kind of capacity this open-endedness is, what it consists in. Furthermore, any creature which possesses this feature must also possess the further capacity to decide when to stop reflecting in this way and come to a firm decision, rather than deliberating indefinitely. This is not possible for a machine in principle either, however: a chess-playing computer, for example, has to 'decide' in a given situation how long to go on considering the pros and cons of a *prima facie* advantageous move.

At this point an objection might be raised to the whole idea that a machine could be capable of the sort of open-ended reflection discussed here. The objection goes as follows. The ability of a machine to reflect on what it is doing, is conceptually limited by the fact that the machine has itself been created for a purpose – a purpose which is not its own. And there is no 'going beyond' that purpose and asking how desirable a purpose it is. The machine logically cannot, on this view, bring into question the ultimate reasons why it does what it does, for they are not *its* reasons. A machine, for instance, which is built for the purpose of working out the series of prime numbers, may well be capable of deliberating up to a point. It may decide, say, to investigate a number which looks a hopeful candidate for being prime; and it might subsequently decide not to do so, on the grounds that if it investigated every number with the same degree of probability of being prime, the job would take too long. But what it cannot do is reach the point at which it begins to say 'What's the good of working out prime numbers in any case?' – for this purpose was not *its* purpose, and we can only deliberate about our *own* purposes.

This objection is very tempting, but in the end will not stand up. It is true that the machines which get built at present do not have the potential to say 'I'm going to stop diagnosing patients and have a game of chess instead'. This is the point about lacking autonomy. It is also true that a machine for diagnosing patients, or for working out square roots, cannot call into question the reasonableness of these activities. But we must be careful about *why* they cannot. It is not, in fact, because the purposes are the purposes of the designer or programmer and not of the machine itself. Rather, it is because it is a simple logical truth that a machine for working out square roots cannot call into question the reasons for its own activity: if it did so, it would be, at least partly, a machine for calling into question its own activity, and not a machine for working out square roots.

Consider a machine which is built for the purpose of simulating human thought. Here, there is no contradiction in supposing that it might question the reasonableness of its own behaviour. Of course, we need to be careful how we express what it is supposed to be doing: a machine which represented to itself its own purpose as that of 'simulating human thought' would be *eo ipso* a failure, since simulation of human thought means simulating what human beings do when they think – and what they do is not 'simulating human thought'! However, this is not a conceptual obstacle, since the only difference between 'simulating human thought' and simply 'thinking the way that human beings do' is what we call them – and the nature of an activity cannot be altered by what someone else calls it. If, then, the machine regarded its task as simply doing what human beings do, there is no reason why it should not bring that activity into question. Some human beings themselves do this: they typically go mad, or commit suicide, or write existentialist novels. This brings us to the second point which was to be discussed in response to the question of how human purposiveness differs from that of machines.

purpose as freedom of the will
If someone says 'How do you know you are not merely like a programmed machine?', it is possible that he intends the question to be synonymous with 'How do you know you have free will?' Freedom of the will is, after all, one meaning of

'autonomy'. A response which I might well make is to appeal to the experience of making a free choice. People have often talked, misleadingly, as though some psychological or sociological discovery might convince us that we lack a property, the property of free will, which we thought we possessed. In the words of another well-known limerick:

> There was a young man who said 'Damn!
> It is clear to me now that I am
> Just a creature that moves
> In predestinate grooves,
> I'm not even a bus, I'm a *tram*!'

The question of free will has often been approached in terms of the absence of constraints. If a person is not at gunpoint, or brainwashed, or whatever, he is free to act as he pleases, and this is what constitutes freedom of will – so the story goes. The application of this principle to the case of automata shows, however, what is basically wrong with the principle as applied to human persons. The mere absence of constraints is not sufficient by itself to make us suspect the presence of true self-motivation, or autonomy. One can imagine many an artifact which is in some way animated, and is not acting under any hindrance or abnormal influence, but is nevertheless a poor candidate for having an autonomous will. The absence of constraints can, then, be only a necessary, and not a sufficient condition for freedom of the will.

What is wrong with the attitude of the young man in the rhyme is that he is looking in the wrong place for the answer to the question about human free will. The person who takes this kind of position considers 'external' circumstances such as the fact that people are made of physical stuff, or that they undergo a process of socialisation, and comes to an absurd conclusion on the basis of them. Why absurd? Because anyone who has had the experience of making a free decision knows that this is what it is, and no amount of drawing attention to background and antecedents is going to alter the fact. To act freely is simply to make a choice. And the way we learn what it is to make a genuine choice – how we learn what the word 'choice' means – is by associating it with actions of just this kind. Nor does this involve committing ourselves to the idea that choice is an occult 'mental act', which many anti-mentalistic philosophers would want to reject, and which is certainly suspect. All we need to accept is that the word 'choice' has a legitimate use. We cannot then be denied the right to say that to experience the making of a choice at first-hand is to have been the agent, in a situation where the word 'choice' is rightly applied.

Two things ought to convince us that the idea of our not really possessing free will, though it seems to us that we do, is incoherent. Firstly, if I do not possess free will, what would it be like to be *really* free? Can we describe a kind of choice freer, say, than my recent choice of a cup of coffee rather than tea? Of course, we could say that a choice made without any causal influence would be freer, but, even granted that we could make any sense of this idea, how would that affect *me*? Hidden constraints which might or might not be there are no constraints at all. To insist nevertheless that I am not free, is like a person claiming that he is imprisoned, though he can't actually point to the walls, and they don't obstruct him in any way. Secondly, suppose that we *do* possess free will, but that we can nevertheless make sense of the idea that we may have turned out not to do. What would this be like? Would we feel our legs and arms acting outside our control, suddenly carrying us where we do not want to go? This idea is equally absurd. But what is wrong with the whole picture, is the confused idea that somehow it is an open question whether or not we ever make genuine choices – that it might turn out one way or the other, and that it is possible to remain open to persuasion either way. The fact is, that if what I have got does not count as free will, then nothing ever would.

Now having – apparently – dispatched free will problem in a couple of pages, it is necessary to point out that this does not get us any further as regards explaining how free will is possible, or how it is brought about. The apparent short shrift given to the problem above was, in fact, *only* apparent; for the real question is this latter. Compare this with the way in which people often mistake the philosopher's question *'How* do I know there is a table in front of me?' for the question '*Do* I know there is a table in front of me?', and regard the philosopher as some sort of crank. What we really want to know is, then: how does it come about that human beings possess autonomy, that they can make genuine choices rather then merely apparent ones? And more acutely, how can we reconcile this with the fact that we are physical creatures living in a physical world obeying physical laws? This, unfortunately, is a perennial problem of philosophy on which there is an enormous literature but very little consensus. Notice also, that this problem is in some ways like that of other minds, in the sense that I have first-hand experience in my own case, but no direct evidence in that of other people: logically speaking, other people could be mere automata without free will, though once again there are *criteria*, though not indefeasible ones, for telling whether a person is really acting freely – and once again, certain things might follow regarding my own case, were I to adopt the sceptical point of view regarding others.

All this bodes rather ill for the prospect of explaining under what circumstances an artifact might be said to possess autonomy, or at what stage in the increasing complexity of machines we ought to be prepared to ascribe genuinely purposive behaviour to them. For on the one hand, the first-hand experience of free choice is one which is only accessible to the agent in question and to no one else: *direct* observation is out of the question. And on the other hand, we are so much in the dark regarding what it is that gives rise to free will in people, that we have little chance of understanding what conditions would give rise to it in artifacts: thus *indirect* evidence is also rendered next door to impossible. All we can do, it seems, is to conclude that the closer machines come to resembling our own structure and organisation, the more reason there will be to suppose them genuinely autonomous. Yet the function of artificial intelligence is surely not to produce an exact duplication of a human being. Nor is there any reason to suppose that *only* our own physical make-up is such as to give rise to the appropriate conditions for autonomy.

Some people have argued that an automaton could by its

very nature never be properly said to be acting autonomously, simply because it is by definition merely doing what it was intended to do by its designer. This, however, conflicts with the principle argued for above, which is that if one is acting freely, one cannot be mistaken about it: for it to be *exactly like* free action simply is for it to *be* free action. Because what this objection entails is that all that is necessary to discredit the idea that something is acting autonomously, is to show that it was designed for a purpose, by someone else, and that it is doing no more than fulfilling that purpose. But there is no contradiction in supposing that we were designed by somebody, with the intention that we should be doing exactly what we are in fact doing. Yet if we were right in thinking that freedom is ensured by the nature of the first-hand experience, then we appear to have a knock-down guarantee against such a discovery! This cannot be right. It seems that mere evidence of design, of derivativeness, is not sufficient to refute the ascription of free will. After all, most people who believe that we were designed, in some sense, by God, do not regard this as excluding the possibility of free will, but rather as the explanation of it.

Finally, if the nature of the first-hand experience of choice and decision – the action as it appears to the agent – is that in which free will ultimately resides, then it appears that only a creature capable of *conscious* thought is going to be a candidate for autonomy. Now it is interesting to see how the features we have been discussing appear to converge. It has been argued that thought, because of the need for concepts, rule-following, and therefore purposiveness, requires autonomy, and that autonomy requires consciousness. If all that has been said is true, we are now in a position to see how the ideas of thinking and consciousness, whose problematical relationship we observed in chapter 1, might be seen as connected. The pattern of entailment will look something like the diagram on the next page.

In the next chapter we will return to the connection between the capacity for genuine thought and the status of being an organism, and tie up some further loose ends from earlier chapters.

THINKING
|
CONCEPTUALISATION
|
RULE-FOLLOWING
|
PURPOSIVENESS
|
AUTONOMY ·
|
CONSCIOUSNESS

11: some conclusions

Continuing to draw threads together, we saw in the last chapter how a genuinely thinking creature would need to be sentient, purely in order to have anything to think about. We saw also that it would require the means to interact with and manipulate its environment. It has further been suggested that such a creature would have to be in the nature of an organism as a result of these preconditions. We will now look at another reason, arising out of the later sections of the last chapter, why this must be so.

more on organisms
If we accept that having purposes is an essential ingredient of the ability to form concepts, then it is appropriate to ask what might be the conditions under which it makes sense to ascribe purposiveness. Towards the end of the last chapter, we discussed two approaches to purposiveness, one in terms of the ability to reflect, and the other in terms of free will. Neither of these led us very far on its own, largely because the properties in question are not well enough understood in the case of human beings, let alone anything else. There is, however, something in addition that can be said on this topic, which is less abstract and more mundane, but which perhaps gets us further in the long run.

To have purposes is to have reasons for doing things. What kind of creatures, then, does it make sense to think of as having reasons? A plausible suggestion is that having reasons depends, at bottom, on having needs. It is hard to see how a creature without any basic needs could, for instance, go on to develop wants, interests and the like. This is not, of course, to say that all our wants and interests *are* really needs; that would be absurd. It is to say that the possibility of having these motivations which are, as it were, at one remove from the basic necessities of life, depends ultimately on being a living creature for whom some basic necessities exist.

Now the concept of needs is by no means an easy one. It enjoys somewhat vague and fuzzy relations with its neighbours, the concepts of *wants* and of *conditions*. For example, it is unclear whether it is correct to say that people need sexual activity as well as needing food, or whether it is something that they just want. They will not die without it, certainly, but it is nevertheless one of the basic stock of strong human impulses which will not go away, and pathological symptoms can result from its repression. On the other hand, a car can, in a sense, be said to need fuel. It will not run without it, and this is in some ways analogous to saying that a human being will not

The car itself is just as satisfied sitting in the middle of the road.

'flourish' without certain things being granted to it. However, it arguably makes more sense to say that it is *we* who need fuel in order to run the car. Fuel is not a need of the car in the same sense that food is a need for us, but only a *condition* of its functioning in the way we want it to. The car itself is just as satisfied sitting motionless in the middle of the road. The crucial difference between this and the case of organisms, is that the latter possess a kind of internal constitution which drives them to seek those things which are necessary for their flourishing. The needs and the drives are, in the case of organisms, internally related to each other, in the sense that the lack is recognized by its resulting in the drive, and the drive can be identified solely in terms of the thing whose lack it points to, and whose presence would be a fulfilment of it. Cars do not, in a sense, have drives – they are merely driven!

back to the original question

In the light of all this, then, what we are to say in answer to the main question which we set ourselves at the outset: *could a machine be really thinking?*

It should be clear that we have come a considerable way towards knowing what an answer to this question is going to look like. Having first asked the question in chapter 1, we went on in chapter 2 to see that it raises problems which have much in common with the traditional philosophical Problem of Other Minds, and that the two may usefully be treated together, which was what happened in chapter 3. In chapter 4 we gave what may be regarded as a fairly standard, present-day response to the Other Minds problem, along Wittgensteinian lines. In chapter 5 we drew out some of the implications of the Wittgensteinian concern with communication, and attained some understanding of what a machine would be required to do in the way of interacting with human beings, before it could be seriously suspected of harbouring a mental life.

At this point, it was decided to glance at various answers to the question of what, in general, is supposed to be the relation between a physical body and the mental life which it possesses – in other words, at the Mind-Body Problem. This we did in chapters 6, 7 and 8. Having reached a broad idea (only one among many defended by various people) of what kind of theory would be acceptable, we went on in chapter 9 to see, in the light of this, how man-made systems compare with human brains as candidates for supporting conscious thought. We will remember that at this stage it looked as though (a) no such system currently in existence would seem to be a very good candidate, but (b) there seemed to be no reason in principle why systems developed in the future should not be, provided we understand that they are still a long way in the future. In chapter 10, however, an argument was given to the effect that purposiveness, autonomy and free will all seem to come into the picture; and we have seen earlier in this chapter how any physical system which fulfils the conditions for genuine thought is almost certainly going to be some kind of organism, because of the apparent connection between purposiveness and the having of needs.

The question now arises: have we narrowed down the conditions under which we are prepared to entertain the idea that something is genuinely thinking, to the point at which machines are ruled out by definition? In other words, are we now committed to answering our original question in the negative, by saying 'No – nothing could be both a machine and fulfil these conditions'?

Frankenstein revisited

This question is not going to be so easy to answer, largely because the word 'machine', as used in this context, is not terribly well defined. We noted near the beginning that a question which can be answered simply by a stipulative definition in no real question at all – so the dictionary will not help us here. A better approach would be to ask: *what, if anything, would be the point of referring to something with the kind of thought-suggesting characteristics we have outlined, as a machine*? One answer might be, simply to record the fact that it is man-made, and not something that occurs spontaneously in nature. Yet plenty of things are man-made and yet are not machines. Another could be, to convey the idea that the thing is non-organic. But in this case the answer to our question would now be trivial, for we have seen that a truly thinking thing is going to be an organism of some sort.

The word 'machine' is, however, sometimes used to signify that the thing in question exists for a purpose or purposes which are external to itself – that is, purposes for others, which are not the purposes of the thing itself (as in the example of the car above). Now on this understanding, it would seem on first sight that it is still going to be false that something could both be a machine and fulfil the conditions for genuinely thinking, since we have argued that purposiveness (involving self-motivation, having its own reasons, etc.) is one of these latter conditions. It is conceivable, however, that a thing should have both purposes of its own and also purposes for which it was designed and built by someone else, and that in such a case it would properly be describable both as a machine in the above sense, and as fulfilling the conditions we laid down.

But what could such a 'machine' be *for*? Surely the only possible kind of reason for creating a machine with purposiveness of its own – unless of course this self-motivation were just a sort of by-product – would be to see whether it could be done, or to find out how it would behave if it *were* done. And this is a somewhat trivial way of being a machine, since the 'machine aspect' of it cannot be described without making reference to its 'non-machine aspect' (i.e. it would be a kind of 'machine-for-being-something-other-than-a- machine'!).

Yet we might, after all, need to take seriously the idea of self-motivation occurring as a by-product. It may be that there could be good reasons for wanting machines which perform tasks which are so complex that any machine capable of performing them would turn out to be so sophisticated, and in just the right ways, that it would in fact be such as to have its own reasons, motives, purposes and so on.

At this point, however, it does look a little as if we are in danger of ending up merely juggling with words. This is not because the results of our enquiry are trivial, but because the real work has already been done. We have, as promised, ended up with an answer, and quite a substantive answer, to the question 'What kind of thing could we take seriously as a candidate for having genuine thought?' The further question of whether or not such a thing could ever be properly called a machine, does not have the same philosophical interest.

What is more interesting, perhaps, is the observation that such artifacts would be hardly anything like the things which pass for 'intelligent machines' at the present time. Even the kinds of system discussed at the end of chapter 9 are hopelessly crude by comparison. This is by no means an attempt to belittle the work done by researchers in Artificial Intelligence in recent years: it is only to point out that, if their goals are those discussed in this book, of creating conscious, thinking beings, then they are perhaps nearer the beginning of the road than the end. We have seen, however, that this is *not* at all the only possible (or actual) aim of Artificial Intelligence. Merely making replicas of ourselves would be at best a pointless, and at worst a perverse and grotesque, task to set ourselves. This is one of the *real* horrors of the Frankenstein story, as opposed to those of its stock Hollywood treatment. The sheer metaphysical audacity of wishing to do such a thing merely to prove that one can do it, is unattractive in itself. And research whose motivation is of this kind rarely results in anything genuinely edifying. Yet, as has been hinted, there may turn out to be perfectly respectable motives which in time will bear fruits in the form of conscious, thinking beings which are at the same time artifacts created by human beings. But this is mere speculation.

Whether or not it is the case, the philosophical questions retain their interest, and can if we wish be pursued as well for their own sake as for any light which they might throw on our technological future. We have, it is to be hoped, also found that in the pursuit of these questions many other interesting lines of enquiry present themselves, some of which are as much to do with ourselves and our own capacity for thought, as with that of our creations.

the indispensability of the philosophical questions
One more, fairly general, position which has been implicitly

argued for in this book, is the following: that a discussion of whether or not machines can be 'really' intelligent or can 'really' think, cannot, in the end, be carried on without reference to the question of whether or not they could be conscious. This is important, since it is often claimed that the questions about genuine thought and intelligence are independent of 'philosophers' questions' about consciousness and the like. On that view, the philosophical questions, though they may retain some academic interest merely for their own sake, are otherwise redundant. But if the argument in chapter 10 is correct, then the questions in which Artificial Intelligence researchers are interested *cannot* be divorced from those which the philosopher insists on asking. For, if we are right, anything which is a proper candidate for having 'real' thought (even in a fairly broad sense) must operate with concepts. And if it is capable of concept-ualisation, this presupposes the ability for rule-following, which itself seems to depend on the presence of purposiveness, which in turn appears to require the possession of autonomy. And we have seen that it is at least quite arguable that a creature can only plausibly be said to be autonomous in this sense if it knows what it is doing, in the fullest sense of this expression, i.e. if it thinks consciously, as opposed to merely 'going through the motions'.

Even questions about whether machines can think in quite weak senses of the word 'think', will tend to get us involved in the above sequence of reasoning. And if this in indeed the case, then it is no longer open for defenders of Artificial Intelligence as 'real', to maintain that the conceptual, philosophical questions can be ignored or shelved, safe in the knowledge that their own questions can stand independently.

suggestions for further reading

Chapter 1
For a variety of approaches to the question of machines and thinking, see Edward A. Feigenbaum and Julian Feldman (eds.) *Computers and Thought* (New York: McGraw-Hill, 1963), which is a collection of articles from various sources. Many other books on the subject are in print, some better than others.

Chapter 2
For more on solipsism and the problem of other minds, see for example the *Proceedings of the Aristotelian Society* supplementary volume 1946 which contains a symposium on the problem of other minds, in which the contributors are John Wisdom, J.L. Austin, and A.J. Ayer. Wisdom's is also reprinted in his book *Other Minds* (Oxford: Blackwell, 1952), and Austin's in Antony Flew (ed.) *Logic and Language*, 2nd series (Oxford: Blackwell, 1953).

Chapter 3
The main primary texts for the material covered in this chapter are as follows: Richard Rorty, *Philosophy and the Mirror of Nature* (New Jersey: Princeton University Press and Oxford: Blackwell, 1981); Daniel Dennett, *Brainstorms* (Montgomery, Vermont: Bradford Books, and Hassocks: Harvester, 1978) ch. 1; Thomas Nagel, 'What is it like to be a Bat?', *Philosophical Review* vol. 83 (Oct.1974), repr. in Nagel, T., *Mortal Questions* (Cambridge: Cambridge University Press, 1979); Bertrand Russell *Human Knowledge: Its Scope and Limits* (London:

Allen & Unwin, 1948); A.J. Ayer, 'One's Knowledge of Other Minds' in Ayer, A.J. (ed.) *Philosophical Essays* (London: Macmillan, 1954), reprinted in Gustafson, D.F. (ed.), *Essays in Philosophical Psychology* (London: Macmillan, 1967). The secondary literature is largely as for chapter 2.

Chapter 4

The primary text here is, of course, Wittgenstein's *Philosophical Investigations* (1953), and especially the part from section 201 to around section 265, where the Private Language Argument and related topics are to be found. A good secondary text is Fogelin's *Wittgenstein*, in the RKP *Arguments of the Philosophers* series. Also useful is Anthony Kenny's *Wittgenstein* (Harmondsworth: Penguin, 1973).

Chapter 5

The classic essay by Turing is contained in the collection edited by Feigenbaum and Feldman (see under ch. 1). On the issue of machines and programs which interact conversationally with human beings, see the relevant sections of Margaret Boden's *Artificial Intelligence and Natural Man* (Hassocks: Harvester Press, 1977) which is a good book for philosophical questions about AI generally, and does not presuppose any technical knowledge.

Chapter 6

The primary texts for this chapter are: Descartes, *Meditations* (1641); Malebranche, *De la Récherche de la Vérité* (6th edn., 1712); Leibniz, *Monadology* (1714); and T.H. Huxley, *Science and Culture* (1881). Annotated readings from the primary literature in the philosophy of mind can be found in Antony Flew (ed.), *Body, Mind, and Death* (London and New York: Macmillan, 1964). On Descartes a good introductory work is Anthony Kenny's *Descartes* (New York: Random House, 1968). On Leibniz, see George MacDonald Ross, *Leibniz* (Oxford: Oxford University Press, 1984). Good articles on the above philosophers, and on many others mentioned in this book, can also be found in F.C. Coplestone's multi-volume

History of Philosophy (London: Burns Oates, 1947-60).

Chapter 7

The primary literature here includes: D.A. Armstrong, *A Materialist Theory of the Mind* (London: Routledge and Kegan Paul, 1968); J.J.C. Smart, 'Sensations and Brain Processes' (*Philosophical Review* 1959); Gilbert Ryle, *The Concept of Mind* (London: Hutchinson, 1949); and Donald Davidson, *Essays on Actions and Events* (Oxford: Oxford University Press, 1980), particularly the essay 'Mental Events' (1970). Some original papers on functionalism are contained in Ned Block (ed.), *Readings in the Philosophy of Psychology* (2 vols. (London: Methuen, 1980)), and Block's introductions are particularly helpful. A good collection of articles, mainly on functionalism and related topics, is J.I. Brio and Robert W. Shahan (eds.), *Mind, Brain and Function* (Norman: University of Oklahoma Press, 1982).

Chapter 8

For this chapter the primary reading is: P.F. Strawson, *Individuals* (London: Methuen, 1959); Bertrand Russell, *Our Knowledge of the External World* (London: Allen and Unwin, 1914) and *The Analysis of Mind* (London: Allen and Unwin, 1921); Spinoza, *Ethics* (c.1666); and Kant's *Critique of Pure Reason* (1781) or his much shorter and easier *Prolegomena* (1783). Some useful secondary literature is: A.J. Ayer, *Russell* (London: Collins, 1972); Stuart Hampshire, *Spinoza* (Harmondsworth: Penguin, revised edn. 1962), and Ralph C.S. Walker, *Kant* (London: Routledge & Kegan Paul, 1978).

Chapter 9

On computers and how they work, a good introduction is Susan Curran and Ray Curnow, *The Penguin Computing Book* (Harmondsworth: Penguin, 1983). For a more advanced account of computer architecture, a classic is V.Carl Hamacher *et al.*, *Computer Organization* (New York: McGraw-Hill, 1984). On Artificial Intelligence see Avron Barr and Edward A. Feigenbaum (eds.), *The Handbook of Artificial Intelligence*

(New York: Pitman, 1981), also Deborah L.S. Sweitzer and Paul- André Schabracq, *Artificial Intelligence: The State of the Art* (Science Council of Canada, 1982). For a layman's introduction to the workings of the human brain, the best text is Colin Blakemore, *Mechanics of the Mind* (Cambridge: Cambridge University Press, 1986).

Chapter 10

For the Chinese Room example, and surrounding issues, see John Searle, *Minds, Brains and Science* (London: BBC Publications, 1986). On the question of sentience a particularly interesting (though perhaps difficult) paper is Daniel Dennett's 'Why You Can't Make a Computer that Feels Pain' in his *Brainstorms*, (q.v. ch. 3, above), ch. 11.

Chapter 11

For further reading on the general subject of this book, two good collections of articles are: J.R. Smythies (ed.), *Brain and Mind: Modern Concepts of the Nature of Mind* (London: Routledge and Kegan Paul, 1965), and Christopher Hookway (ed.), *Minds, Machines and Evolution* (Cambridge: Cambridge University Press, 1984).

glossary of names

Armstrong, D.M. (b. 1926)
Australian philosopher whose best-known work is *A Materialist Theory of the Mind*, in which he defends a form of Central State Materialism (see chapter 7).

Ayer, Sir A.J. (b. 1910)
The principal British exponent of Logical Positivism, a school of thought which was concerned to lay down criteria distinguishing the meaningful from the nonsensical. His book *Language, Truth and Logic* (1936) laid down a central thesis of Logical Positivism, which was that a statement is only factually meaningful if there is, in principle, some means of verifying it, i.e. of discovering when it is true.

Berkeley, George (1685-1753)
Emphiricist philosopher, who was also an Irish Bishop. Berkeley took empiricism (the school of philosophy which emphasised sense experience as the source of knowledge) to its limits, by arguing that there are only 'ideas' in the mind (e.g. sensations), and that material things have no real existence. This is a form of Idealism (see chapter 7).

Brentano, Franz (1838-1917)
German philosopher/psychologist who was the founder of that school of philosophy known as Phenomenology. In his book *Psychology from an Empirical Standpoint* (1874), he originated the concept of 'intentionality' (see chapter 3).

Davidson, Donald (b. 1930)

American philosopher, very influential since the late 1960s. His views are very difficult to summarise, but are largely contained in his books *Essays On Actions and Events* (1980) and *Inquiries into Truth and Interpretation* (1984).

Dennett, Daniel (b. 1942)

American philosopher of mind. His views are not easy to summarise, but are contained in his books *Content and Consciousness* (1969) and *Brainstorms* (1978).

Descartes, René (1596-1650)

French philosopher, probably now best known for his *Meditations*, in which he attempted to reconstruct the framework of human knowledge. In his philosophy of mind he was a dualist, believing mind and body to be two separate entities, or 'substances'. Among other things, Descartes believed that the existence of God could be rationally demonstrated.

Fodor, J.A.

American philosopher best known for his work in semantics with J.J. Katz, but who has also written on the philosophy of mind, taking a functionalist position (see chapter 7).

Fichte, J.G. (1762-1814)

German philosopher whose system of philosophy owes much to Kant, whilst departing from Kant's views in many important respects. In Fichte's account the primary source of knowledge is the self, or ego, which constructs the world for itself out of a collection of 'appearances'.

Hegel, G.W.F. (1770-1831)

Along with Kant (q.v.) the best-known of the German idealists. Hegel's vast and comprehensive system of philosophy is known as Absolute Idealism. His style is dense and obscure, making his work very difficult for a layman to approach.

Husserl, Edmund (1859-1938)
Along with Brentano, a founder of the school of philosophy known as Phenomenology, which attempts to proceed from closely and objectively observed data of consciousness, and working from these towards a general theory of knowledge.

Huxley, T.H. (1825-1895)
Scientist and philosopher whose main contribution to philosophy has probably been the theory of mind known as Epiphenomenalism (see chapter 6).

James, William (1842-1910)
American psychologist and philosopher, one of the chief exponents (along with Dewey and Peirce) of the school of philosophy known as Pragmatism. His theory of the relation between the mental and the physical, known as neutral monism, was taken up by Bertrand Russell (q.v.).

Kant, Immanuel (1724-1804)
One of the most influential philosophers of all time. Kant developed a system of philosophy known as Transcendental Idealism, which is laid out in his most celebrated work, the *Critique of Pure Reason* (1781). It is probably no exaggeration to say that all modern philosophy owes something to Kant.

Kripke, Saul (b. 1942)
American philosopher, whose main work lies in logic, philosophy of language and metaphysics. He has argued against the materialist account of mind (see chapter 7).

Leibniz, Gottfried Wilhelm (1646-1716)
German philosopher, along with Descartes (q.v.) and Spinoza (q.v.) one of the three great Rationalist philosophers. Attempted to reconcile a mechanistic, scientific account of the world, with a teleological (i.e. purposive) theological understanding. He created a system of metaphysics in which the ultimate entities are non-interacting 'monads'.

Malebranche, Nicholas (1638-1715)
French philosopher, much influenced by Descartes (q.v.), but who espoused a theory of mind and body known as Occasionalism (see chapter 6).

Putnam, Hilary (b. 1926)
American philosopher, notable for his work in metaphysics and philosophy of science. His best-known works are contained in his volumes of collected papers. Putnam's large and fertile output has influenced many present-day philosophers.

Rorty, Richard
American philosopher who has advocated the rejection of much traditional metaphysics and philosophy of mind. Rorty's views are hard to summarise, but are to be found in his three main works: *The Linguistic Turn* (1967), *Consequences of Pragmatism* (1982), both collections of articles, and *Philosophy and the Mirror of Nature* (1980).

Russell, Bertrand (1872-1970)
The most famous English philosopher of the twentieth century. His most celebrated work, written with Alfred North Whitehead, was the *Principia Mathematica* (1910-13), an investigation into the foundations of mathematics. Later he went on to write in most branches of philosophy, and published many popular works besides those intended for the specialist philosopher.

Ryle, Gilbert (1900-76)
Influential Oxford philosopher whose best-known work is *The Concept of Mind* (1949), in which he attacks the idea of an immaterial mind, which he calls the 'myth of the Ghost in the Machine'.

Skinner, B.F. (b. 1904)
Behavioural psychologist whose work has frequently spilled over into philosophy. A believer in the value of deliberate behavioural conditioning of human beings, his most important work from a philosophical point of view is *Beyond Freedom and*

Dignity (1971).

Smart, J.J.C.
Australian philosopher who has written extensively on the philosophy of science and metaphysics. Along with Armstrong (q.v.), he is central state materialist.

Spinoza, Benedict or Baruch (1632-77)
Jewish philosopher who developed a system of metaphysics which he articulated in a deductive form, using axiomatic method as in geometry. Spinoza was a pantheist, believing God and nature to be ultimately identical, and was excommunicated from the Jewish religion as a result of his unorthodox views.

Strawson, Peter F. (b. 1919)
Oxford philosopher whose work is much influenced by Kant (q.v.). His major works are *Individuals* (1959) and *The Bounds of Sense* (1966).

Turing, Alan (1912-54)
More a scientist and mathematician than a philosopher, Turing was instrumental in developing some of the first computers, around the time of the Second World War. His reflections on minds and machines, especially the famous 'Turing Test' (see chapter 5) have, however, provided an interesting focus of discussion for philosophers.

Wittgenstein, Lugwig (1889-1951)
Possibly the most influential philosopher of the twentieth century. Wittgenstein's works are difficult for the layman: the best known of them are the *Tractatus Logico-Philosophicus* (1921) and the *Philosophical Investigations* (posthumus, 1953). Each of these works sets out a system of philosophy, though his views had altered considerably between writing the former and the latter.

Index